CHURCHES OF
NEWCASTLE AND
NORTHUMBERLAND

A SENSE OF PLACE

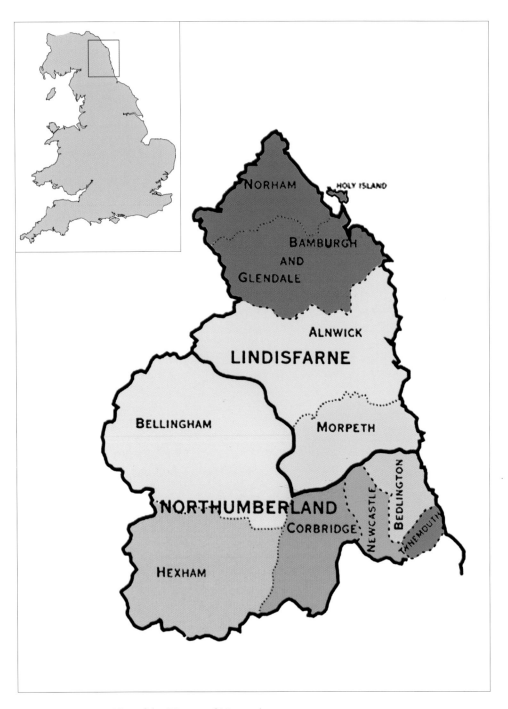

Frontispiece: Map of the Diocese of Newcastle

CHURCHES OF
NEWCASTLE AND
NORTHUMBERLAND

A SENSE OF PLACE

GEOFFREY PURVES

TEMPUS

The churches described in this book are those in the Diocese of Newcastle, Church of England.

First published 2006

Tempus Publishing Limited
The Mill, Brimscombe Port,
Stroud, Gloucestershire, GL5 2QG
www.tempus-publishing.com

© Geoffrey Purves, 2006

British Library Cataloguing in Publication Data.
A catalogue record for this book is available from the British Library.

ISBN 0 7524 4071 3

Typesetting and origination by Tempus Publishing Limited
Printed in Great Britain

CONTENTS

FOREWORD

The views expressed in this book represent many different aspects of life in the Diocese of Newcastle. It is fitting, therefore, that we have endorsements from the Bishop of Newcastle, the Duchess of Northumberland and Newcastle United footballer Shola Ameobi. They all in their own way contribute to the quality of life in our area and help to establish 'a sense of place'. I thank each of them for their support. (Ed.)

I sometimes tell my fellow bishops that none of them has a lovelier part of England to live and work in than I have. Again and again a significant feature of the landscape of city, town and country is a parish church. There are many outstanding examples to be found here and I hope this book will lead you to visit and to explore the treasures we enjoy in this Diocese of Newcastle.

Through it I hope you will be led to enjoy more fully the beauty of these churches, to see how they have developed as buildings over the years, to learn how they have influenced and played a part in the lives of people (ordinary and not so ordinary, the famous as well as the unknown), to catch in them something of the vision of God which inspired their building and still sustains people in their quest for the meaning of life through prayer and worship today.

Whether a church building is over a 1000 years old or only six months old (and we have examples of both in the diocese) it tells a story, a story about the beliefs and the lives, the hopes and the challenges of the people and communities who worship within them.

Churches are places which enable people to meet each other, and to meet God. They are places for declaring love, for seeking consolation in grief, for expressing thanksgiving, for celebrating new life, for sharing sorrows and joys and for dedicating ourselves to, and seeking sustenance from, God.

In our churches, the Christian gospel of God's love for everyone can be found portrayed in stained glass and carved wood, in stone slabs and hanging banners. The joys and sorrows of Christian people can be seen in headstones and memorials, in dedications, in generous gifts and in requests for prayer.

I am immensely grateful to Geoffrey Purves and to all those who have contributed to these pages. This book is a fitting tribute to the first 125 years of the life of this Diocese of Newcastle and I pray that through the essays, the descriptions of all the churches in the diocese and the suggested trails to explore, you will be enabled to discover for yourself the treasures we enjoy in this land of the northern saints.

My hope is that you will appreciate the beauty, charm and craftsmanship of these wonderful buildings, that you will see the care lavished on them by past and present generations of Christian people, and that you will reflect too on the continuous prayer and praise that have been offered in them over so many generations and so be led yourself to 'worship the Lord in the beauty of holiness'.

+ Martin Newcastle

Rt Revd Martin Wharton, Bishop of Newcastle

The rich heritage of Northumbria is available to us all today, in the settlements which reveal our pre-historic antecedents, in the remains of the Roman civilisation which flourished here, in the castles, fortified mansions and pele towers which tell of our turbulent past, and not least in the churches which recall the story of Christianity's earliest beginnings in this part of the world, and give witness to a continuing life of faith and worship. Churches are much more than buildings and monuments, however. They chart the ebb and flow of communities, they speak of changing circumstances and times, and yet they still convey a vital sense of place, a place we can visit and revisit and always hope to find something new and undiscovered.

Her Grace, Jane, Duchess of Northumberland

The North-East is a fantastic place to live, work and enjoy yourself, and if you love football, there's no better place to be. If you also love churches, and you're interested in history, then this place has even more going for it. Wonderful scenery, superb buildings, and some great stories about the saints who established Christianity in this region and helped put Northumbria on the map. This book gives a flavour of that very special atmosphere and shows you where to find it.

Shola Ameobi

ACKNOWLEDGEMENTS

The idea for this book came from the work done on a regular basis by the Diocesan Advisory Committee (DAC). This committee, part of the Newcastle Diocesan administration process, deals with all the changes and alterations to the 200 or so churches in the diocese under the Ecclesiastical Exemption Legislation. It administers the legal framework for church buildings that operates outside the normal secular planning system. The Church of England is, therefore, in the very special position of being the guardian of its own building stock and much of the day-to-day maintenance falls within the voluntary work of churchwardens.

A very useful guidebook was published in 1982, which gives a brief description of all the churches in the Newcastle Diocese, and this publication has proved to be an invaluable reference book but is now out of date. In celebration of the 125th anniversary of the Newcastle Diocese it seemed timely to reconsider the role of churches today.

With encouragement from the Bishop of Newcastle, the Rt Revd Martin Wharton, material for this book has been assembled over the last year or so. Every parish was asked to supply material for the gazetteer. This was collated by Helen Savage, who also helped to prepare the book for publication. Sharon Brown too gave me much valuable assistance. I discussed the approach to the material that follows with people who were involved in the production of the first guidebook, including Richard Ford and Stanley Prins. Sue Scott, a colleague from Diocesan Church House, helped to ensure our planning meetings took place regularly and provided invaluable advice.

I am especially grateful to the Duchess of Northumberland and to Shola Ameobi for their support of this publication which I hope will have wide appeal to anyone interested in the role of churches in our environment. I would also like to thank our individual authors for their valuable contributions and observations about the background and framework of the diocese and especially the role of its church buildings. A number of other people have also contributed generously to the making of this book by suggesting text, amongst whom I would especially like to thank Robin Dower. Some photographs were submitted by the parishes of the diocese. Others are the work of John Rowley, Katy Savage, Helen Savage, Eddie Tingate, Dagmar Winter and Bernard McCabe.

At the end of the book you will find a list of sponsors. Their generous donations have enabled the photographs and illustrations to be printed in colour. I would like to thank them for their support.

Finally, it is important to acknowledge the role of the Archdeacon of Lindisfarne, Bob Langley, and the Archdeacon of Northumberland, Geoff Miller, who, on a day-to-day basis, routinely deals with the endless queries and problems that parishes need to resolve to keep their churches in good order.

Geoffrey Purves

INTRODUCTION

A SENSE OF PLACE

GEOFFREY PURVES

This book marks the 125th anniversary of the Anglican Diocese of Newcastle. It is designed to be a resource to help you to enjoy better the wonderful heritage of church buildings in our region and to learn more about the communities they reflect and serve. I hope that some of the more reflective essays here will also encourage a wide range of people with different interests in these buildings, be they cultural, historical, touristic or religious, to think about how they may best continue to be enjoyed and to be used for the benefit of the whole community.

In this book you will find contributions from people who live and work in the North-East and who know its church buildings well. The first four chapters reflect the special nature of the Church and of church buildings in the North-East of England. Ian Wood begins with a brief but authoritative account of the region's Christian history from the days of Roman Britain to the establishment of Durham Cathedral by the community of St Cuthbert. The legacy of Aidan, Cuthbert, Bede and the many other great saints of what some still regard as the 'golden age' of Northumbrian Christianity continues to exercise a powerful influence on today's Church. This forms the starting point for Christopher Lewis's thought-provoking essay on the nature of spirituality in contemporary society and its relationship to Christian tradition. The discussion is widened by Peter Robinson who offers a fascinating analysis of the social, economic and cultural context in which the Newcastle Diocese finds itself in the early part of the twenty-first century. Finally, in this part of the book, Christopher Dalliston, the Dean of Newcastle, provides a case-study survey of how the Anglican churches in central Newcastle are learning to respond with imagination to this fast-changing culture.

In the middle of the book, Cyril Winskell has contributed four 'tourist' trails – two urban and two rural – two on foot and two which demand transport on two or four wheels – a series of personal views of the place of churches in the landscape, and of the human and natural landscape which has, in turn, influenced those buildings themselves. There is a map to accompany each trail and also watercolours by Cyril Winskell, specially prepared for this book.

Church buildings offer much to see (and indeed to engage all the senses). Neil Moat provides a detailed and thorough guide to stained glass and other fittings. Helen Savage adds some notes about churchyards and gravestones – not quite as morbid a subject as one might imagine. Howard Smith surveys the bells of the diocese and John Roper contributes a personal appreciation of the music-making that takes place in our churches.

The rest (and largest part) of the book is a historical and architectural gazetteer of all the church buildings of the Anglican Diocese of Newcastle, currently used for worship – along with a photograph of each one.

If you wish to study the architectural history of places in the region in greater detail than you will find in the gazetteer here, then there is no better starting-point than the Northumberland edition of Pevsner's authoritative guide to The Buildings of England.[1] Pevsner provides a comprehensive review of the architectural history of church buildings from pre-history and the earliest vernacular styles through to twentieth-century buildings. The Saxon period is better represented in Northumberland than most other English counties and some of the most impressive remains include Bolam, Bywell St Andrew, Corbridge, Ovingham, Warden and Whittingham.

Richard Taylor's How to Read a Church[2] provides a fascinating explanation of what to look for in a church. Simon Jenkins's England's Thousand Best Churches[3] includes a personal selection of outstanding buildings in the North-East and captures the region's special sense of place. I believe that it is this that we should build on in order to open up our rich heritage and valuable asset to a wider audience.

A large number of churches were built in the nineteenth century in south Northumberland and reflect the huge increase in population as a result of the industrial revolution. This continued into the first half of the twentieth century with the development of suburban estates. Since then, the rate of new church building has steadily declined to a mere trickle of what was happening a hundred years ago. Although a smaller number of new buildings are being commissioned, a great deal of work is being undertaken on reordering and thinking afresh about how existing buildings can be used more effectively, efficiently and beneficially as flexible spaces for worship and for the benefit of the wider community – every day of the week. As society becomes more fluid, open and mobile, this trend is to be encouraged.

For more than 5000 years, architecture has expressed and reflected the whole spectrum of human spiritual and emotional needs. The power of buildings to satisfy these needs continues today. Recent debate in the Synod in the Diocese of Newcastle (the local policy-forming forum of the Church of England) has confirmed the importance that people place on church buildings. Many new opportunities are emerging as a result of greater wealth and improved communications to experience a wide range of buildings which have often been underused in the last few decades, and many people are becoming aware of the benefits of opening up the heritage of church buildings to the local community and to visitors. These challenges vary widely from churches threatened with redundancy to major historical and cultural sites. The exciting objective is to secure the preservation of this ecclesiastical built heritage and to bring wider appreciation of its architectural, historical, cultural and social significance to a larger number of people.

There are encouraging signs that new ways are being found to open up these opportunities. Funding is always a problem, but English Heritage has recently launched Inspired, a new campaign which sets out a range of ideas confirming that the government is concerned about the care of our historic places of worship.[4] English Heritage asserts that, 'the best way to secure their future is if they can remain living buildings at the heart of communities, visited, valued and enjoyed by all'.[5] Regional agencies, including One NorthEast, and the major local authorities are preparing cultural strategies.

Culture, which I understand to include a wide range of social, historical and environmental factors, often seems to focus on popular lifestyle activities. The North-East is known as a good place for entertainment and football. St James's Park, home of Newcastle United, dominates Newcastle's skyline in much the same way that Gothic cathedrals tower over many European cities. What can we learn from these cultural influences? What has shaped our wider cultural heritage? Early Christianity helped to shape the landscape; fierce medieval battles gave us fortified architectural monuments and more recently the industrial revolution and the expansion of our cities in the nineteenth and twentieth centuries have influenced today's attitudes. The Church continues to be a vital component in any townscape analysis, but we have allowed church buildings to be underused. They are often undervalued by the surrounding local communities. Many important buildings have suffered and are now 'at risk'. There are, however, some striking examples of the ways in which even these buildings can be reordered to serve new needs.

Other imaginative responses are being put forward, not just for the benefit of local communities but also for a wider range of cultural and heritage explorations by tourists. Tourist shops, for example, provide local commercial opportunities for churches to develop their income, and thereby help to fund essential repair work. Such self-help approaches are encouraged by English Heritage and the government, even though financial assistance to support them is limited.

In 2004 the Church of England published the report Building Faith in our Future, which set out the opportunities and challenges in church buildings in the United Kingdom. It pays special attention to the funding and planning decisions that are of importance for places of worship 'as part of the historic environment which is important to our society and as a physical focus of community activity'.[6]

Building Faith in our Future highlights the importance of working closely with regional cultural consortia and development agencies and recommends that the local strategic partnerships should include representatives from faith communities. Church buildings should be seen as a catalyst to stimulate regeneration of urban areas, and local authorities are encouraged to look to churches as partners in tackling rural exclusion. For example, rural churches can provide crucial services to local communities through the imaginative use of their buildings, land, spaces, people, ideas and energy. They may help to give a voice to many groups, including women, the elderly, the young, ethnic minorities and those with special needs,[7] but it is often far from easy to find the funds to enable such hopes to be realised.

In a speech in September 2003 to those charged with the care of church buildings, the Bishop of London claimed that, 'the Church of England is, in financial terms, the most disestablished Church in western Europe.'

The United Kingdom contributes less towards the upkeep of church buildings than most of our European partners. It grants tax relief (VAT) for repairs to places of worship that are listed buildings (but only to those). It also funds the Churches Conservation Trust, which maintains churches no longer used for regular worship but which are of special historical or architectural merit. The Historic Churches Preservation Trust (HCPT) founded in 1953 has passed on more than £26 million raised from voluntary giving. It helps approximately 300 churches a year distributing around £1.5 million in grants and loans. English Heritage and the Heritage Lottery Fund administer a limited grant scheme for some repairs but again this only applies to churches that are listed buildings. Many do not qualify for help at all.

There is considerable need for the UK government to give English Heritage the money to help the denominations to maintain and develop the use of church buildings more adequately. Here in the North-East we must continue to work with our regional agencies and to build on the opportunities for joint ventures and initiatives in the culture, tourist and heritage areas.

One existing initiative has been undertaken by the Anglican Dioceses of Newcastle and Durham, who are working together to review the role of tourism in the region and see how the Church of England may play its part in this. Other special initiatives by the Newcastle Diocese include a task group on tourism and another which has investigated the most appropriate and imaginative ways to preserve and to use church buildings for the benefit of the whole community. A range of tourist trail brochures has also been published in north Northumberland.

The Regional Tourist Board has been absorbed into the regional development agency, One NorthEast. It wishes to promote a rapid expansion of tourism. To this end, One NorthEast has established four Area Tourism Partnerships. The Berwick Local Strategic Partnership is considering bidding for World Heritage Site status, specifically to include the Christian heritage of the area.

The concept of 'social capital' has recently become important in shaping economic and social policy. It is an attempt to describe those less tangible assets possessed by communities which yet are crucial in making them what they are. Social capital has to do with the level of trust, reciprocity, skills and abilities; cultural character embedded within a community. Those things provide its glue, its corporate identity and its power.

Recently there has been increasing interest in the relevance of this concept for faith communities, and the idea of religious/spiritual capital is being promoted. A working definition of 'religious capital' drawn from some research by the William Temple Foundation is 'the combined total of a church's or faith group's contribution to civil society comprising the interplay between its values, language, methods of engagement and theology'. Religious capital sits within the broader concept of social capital, giving it distinctive directions and dimensions. Religious capital is also much to do with human flourishing and with creativity, reconciliation, wellbeing and happiness.

While the focus on the idea of religious capital has so far been primarily urban, it applies to every context. In rural Northumberland it may take the form of living Christian communities, which by their activities often add to creativity and wellbeing in the area; of buildings which express the distinctive Christian heritages and of histories, often hidden, which have been significant in shaping the culture of the country as a whole.[8]

If churches are to respond positively to the opportunities set out briefly here then the buildings themselves must change. Physically, we need to be more open in considering the reordering of internal spaces to increase flexibility and to accommodate a wider range of activities, many of which may be secular. More people should be invited to become involved in the running of the building and local community groups should be encouraged to think of alternative uses for church buildings. Opportunities exist to develop music, theatre and other performance events. Churches also need to develop further their connections with local authorities and regional bodies. Many of these changes will require permission from diocesan chancellors, advised by Diocesan Advisory Committees, which oversee the planning system in each Anglican Diocese. These, in turn, need to respond positively and with encouragement so that this broader network of relationships can flourish.

ONE

ECCLESIASTICAL ORIGINS BETWEEN THE TEES AND THE TWEED

IAN WOOD

Christianity first came to Britain during the Roman period. By the end of the fourth century, indeed, the Empire was officially Christian, and pagan worship was banned. In an area as firmly under the Roman military authorities as northern Britannia, the Christian Church must have been a significant presence. Even so, archaeologists have been hard pushed to identify churches or other indications of Roman Christianity in the vicinity of Hadrian's Wall. Nor is there anything to prove that the British population was Christian either during the last years of imperial rule or in the ensuing centuries – although it is inconceivable that there were no Christian Britons in the area. There must even be a strong possibility that there was still a Christian presence in the area between the Tees and the Forth when the English kingdom of Northumbria was first established in the sixth century. Certainly, to judge by the few modern assessments of skeletal material, the population of Northumbria is likely to have been largely made up of indigenous Britons. Even so, our knowledge of Christianity in the region begins with the reign of King Edwin, who converted following his marriage to the Kentish princess Æthelburh. He was baptised, according to Bede, in 627.

Edwin's power-base lay in the southern part of his kingdom, in the York region. As a result, much of what we know about the promotion of Christianity in Northumbria during his reign relates to that region, to York itself and to Catterick. Bede, however, who is our main source, tells of Paulinus, the Roman missionary who accompanied Æthelburh, preaching and baptising for 36 days at Yeavering, by the river Glenn. Bede's account has been enhanced by the discoveries of archaeologists who have revealed a major palace-complex at the site which must have been in use during Edwin's reign.

It is unclear what religion had been practised by the pagans whom Paulinus baptised. Bede mentions some of the standard gods of the Germanic pantheon: Tiw, Woden, Thor, who gave their names to the days of the week: Tuesday, Wednesday and Thursday: and the less known Eostre, who gave her name to Easter. But there may have been other cults favoured by the descendants of the troops who had been stationed on the Wall and who had worshipped the *Deae Matres*, the Mother-Goddesses of the Rhineland, as well as Mithras and the better-known members of the Roman pantheon. Even more significant may have been gods associated with specific places: for instance the British god Cocidius, whose cult seems to have been primarily at Bewcastle. More important these may simply have been the powers of nature. Probably the Christian missionaries were not faced with any widespread religious organisation: there is little evidence for either temples or a pagan priesthood.

Edwin ruled only a short period after his conversion, being killed in 633 at the battle of Hatfield Chase, on the moorland of the lower Trent Valley. According to Bede, Christianity suffered a significant setback as a result. Paulinus took the queen south to safety, and only his associate, James the Deacon, remained to keep the mission alive. In Bede's narrative, at least, Christianity had to be reintroduced by Oswald, who took the throne two years after Edwin's death. Whereas the missionaries of Edwin's reign came from Canterbury in Kent, and ultimately indeed from Rome, those of Oswald's reign were Irishmen from the island monastery of Iona, which had been founded by Columba in 565. Oswald had been converted among the Irish settled in western Scotland, and it was to them that he turned for missionaries after he became king of Northumbria. The first missionary unfortunately proved to be unequal to the task, but he was followed by Aidan, who was to be one of the great missionary figures of the early Middle Ages.

Bede presents a remarkable picture of Aidan travelling through the kingdom preaching, initially with the help of interpreters, because of course his native language was Irish. On occasion the king himself is said to have translated for him. In many respects Bede presents Aidan as a model pastoral figure: the one significant criticism he has to offer is that the Irishman calculated the date of Easter in a manner that Bede thought was heretical. For the most part, however, he has nothing but praise for the bishop who travelled on foot, preaching the Gospel. Bede presents other of his heroes as coming from a similar mould: like Aidan, Cuthbert is seen as an ideal pastor, although in the end he retired to be a hermit on Inner Farne. This model of pastoral leadership is set out by Bede in a more programmatic form in the letter he wrote to Bishop Ecgbert of York in 734.

While Aidan and Cuthbert were great evangelists, bishops and pastors, they were also monks, based at the island community of Lindisfarne. Oswald, whose own preferred residence seems to have been at Bamburgh, granted Lindisfarne to Aidan. The peculiar nature of the site suited the needs of Aidan well. It was near the royal palace, indeed it is visible from Bamburgh, but it was also cut off, twice a day, quite literally, by the tide. It was thus both at the heart of the kingdom and set apart from it. This mixture of accessibility and separation balances the combination of pastor and monk in Aidan's own life. It is also to be found more generally in the early medieval Church.

The evidence for pastoral organisation in the period before the twelfth century does not suggest that it followed a carefully imposed scheme. Rather, it developed out of the pastoral work of individuals like Aidan and Cuthbert, and out of the response of leading laymen to that work. What we hear about are the evangelical journeys of the two saints and their like and the estates that were granted to them. We also learn a little about the responsibilities of the clergy, over such matters as preaching, baptism, communion and burial – though most of this evidence is to be found in the canons of councils held in the kingdom of Mercia. In addition we learn about the cults of saints, focused on tombs of men like Cuthbert, which themselves played a significant role in promoting Christianity among the local, and not so local, population, who travelled in search of cures or other sorts of miraculous help.

Because much, if not all, pastoral work was associated with monastic houses, the clearest indication we have of the spread of the Church is to be found in the histories of individual monastic communities, and in particular of Lindisfarne. In the tenth or perhaps the eleventh century a history of the community of St Cuthbert was written up. By that time the monks had left Lindisfarne as a result of the Viking threat, and had travelled through much of Northumbria, pausing in particular at Norham and Chester-le-Street. In 995 the community moved on to its final resting-place of Durham. Whoever composed the so-called History of St Cuthbert (*Historia de Sancto Cuthberto*) would seem to have had access to the community's archives, and he could thus list the grants made by various kings to the community. As a result we find reference to a considerable number of places held by the community of St Cuthbert. Most, if not all, of these must have had some provision for Christian worship. There were major grants to the bishops of Lindisfarne of estates on the mainland opposite Holy Island itself, around Whittingham, Edlingham and on the River Bowmont, as well as much further afield: Cartmel to the south of the Lake District and Crayke to the north of York. On some estates churches are explicitly mentioned; for instance Bishop Ecgred (830-45) built a church at Gainford and gave it to the community. Such churches were staffed by priests, who we may guess were attached to the monastic community. Some of them may have lived in the monastery, or in one of its dependent communities, and travelled out when necessary to officiate in a chapel or church.

We know more about early gifts to Lindisfarne than to other monastic houses because the community of St Cuthbert survived and developed into that of Durham. We can, however, see a similar pattern of gift and pastoral provision in the case of a handful of other monasteries. Something of the holdings of the great monasteries founded by Wilfrid at Hexham and Ripon is recorded in the life of the saint written by Stephen in the early eighth century. After the division of the large Northumbrian Diocese in 678, Hexham, like Lindisfarne, became the seat of a bishop, who must have had an eye to pastoral responsibilities. The church still boasts its Anglo-Saxon *frith* stool (which may have been the bishop's chair) and its splendid crypt built by Wilfrid, in part to provide pilgrims with access to relics that Wilfrid had brought back from Rome.

Like the bishops, the abbots of the leading monasteries would have been concerned with the provision of pastoral care for clerics and monks attached to the community and indeed for estate workers on their property. Bede provides information on early grants to Wearmouth (founded *c*.673) and Jarrow (founded *c*.681) in his *Life of the Abbots*, while some of his exegetical works and homilies throw light on the presence of laymen to be found in the congregations at some church services. Given the fact that the larger monastic communities had several churches, separate provision could have been made, at least in some instances, for laity and the monks or nuns. At Jarrow one eighth-century chapel survives complete, in the chancel of the present parish church, while Monkwearmouth still boasts its pre-Viking western porch and tower. Bede, however, is not our only source for the estates of Wearmouth-Jarrow, which are more fully recorded in the *Historia de Sancto Cuthberto*, because a significant number of them were given to the community of St Cuthbert in the course of the Viking invasions. As a result it is possible to reconstruct the Bishop Wearmouth estate south of the Wear.

The evidence for Lindisfarne, or rather the community of St Cuthbert, and for Hexham, Wearmouth and Jarrow provides the fullest insights into the early Church of the northern part of Northumbria – a Church dominated by monasteries, which seem to have taken over most of the duties of pastoral care in the region. There were other monasteries, some of them of considerable importance, but we know much less about them even though they were founded by or associated with royalty: there was the nunnery at Coldingham on St Abb's Head and the monastery at Tynemouth, which was a burial place of kings. There was another monastery at South Shields, which was handed over to nuns, and a nunnery on the Wear, once ruled by Abbess Hild, which may have been transferred to Wearmouth. Particularly interesting is a community which is the subject of a ninth-century poem called the *De Abbatibus* (About the Abbots). It may have been based at Bywell on the Tyne, which boasts two important Anglo-Saxon churches. The poem is all the more interesting in that it provides a vivid picture of life in a monastery which was not one of the great foundations of the period.

There were plenty of other foundations which were rather less distinguished. We learn about them from Bede's letter to Ecgbert. Land in early Anglo-Saxon authority was largely, if not entirely, in the power of the king, who granted it to followers in return for military service. On the follower's death the land returned to the king. There were, in other words, no hereditary estates. This pattern of land-holding was, however, problematic for the Church, which needed land in perpetuity. As a result kings started to alienate property by means of written charters. Not surprisingly, it was not long before laymen saw in church-foundation the possibility of securing property for their families in perpetuity. As a result, in the early eighth century according to Bede, individual laymen started to petition the king for land on which to found monasteries. This they did, but having done so they and their families continued to live in the new foundations. Bede condemns these families, or bogus monasteries, as they have been called by historians, and encouraged Bishop Ecgbert to take some of them over, turning them into pastoral centres within his diocese. It is possible that some reform did take place. It is, however, also clear that, despite Bede's objections to these foundations, they were centres where monks could be found and where the liturgy was practised. They could have developed into proprietary churches, controlled by individual landowners but nevertheless providing pastoral care for the estates on which they were based.

It is not clear whether any of these family monasteries have left any physical remains. The stone church at Escomb is likely to have been monastic in origin – but it is a building of such quality that it is likely to have been associated with a community. Some of the numerous fragments of Anglo-Saxon stone sculpture which are to be found throughout the Northumbrian region could come from family monasteries. The great pillar at Bewcastle, for instance, seems to be the product of a monastic community, and its inscription suggests that it was associated with a group of aristocrats. Unfortunately there are no written records to elucidate the history of this or any other equivalent site.

With the exception of the community of St Cuthbert, no Northumbrian monastery has left any documentation from the period between the mid-ninth century and the Norman Age. In the twelfth century we see the establishment of a much more coherent system of diocesan and parish organisation, much of it imposed from above. Below the cathedral community of Durham there were a number of minster or mother churches, whose significance may have derived from the earlier period. In looking for continuity with the age of Bede, however, one needs to remember the impact of the Viking raids. Not that there had been major Scandinavian settlement north of the Tees. Indeed, something of the Northumbrian kingdom lasted in the so-called Lordship of Bamburgh up into the eleventh century. Above all, the community of St Cuthbert not only survived but in certain respects it prospered. Admittedly the monks abandoned Lindisfarne, and set out on their wanderings that would take them to Norham, Chester-le-Street and finally Durham. But, unlike any other community, it did manage to keep their major treasures: above all the relics of Cuthbert and their manuscripts, especially the *Lindisfarne Gospels*. It also kept hold of many of their estates, and could still lay claim to them in the twelfth century. It even acquired the property of some other houses which had fared less well. It seems to have taken over some of the manuscripts and lands of Wearmouth-Jarrow. The land between the Tyne and the Wear was supposedly given to the community by a Viking king, Guthred, whose relations with the Bishop Eardwulf appear to have been remarkably cordial.

As a result, Durham, the final resting-place of the community of St Cuthbert, boasts greater links with the pre-Viking past than does any other religious establishment in the northernmost part of England. Other monastic houses failed, were destroyed or were subsumed into the community of Cuthbert. Looking back from the eleventh and twelfth centuries, churchmen saw a period of devastation – though they may well have exaggerated it, in order to highlight their own achievements in restoring what they saw as the Golden Age of the seventh and eighth centuries. That the pre-Viking Age was remarkable, however, is certain. Ecclesiastical provision and a pastoral system had been established throughout Northumbria, even if in a somewhat haphazard way, dependent on the vagaries of monastic foundation and endowment. Moreover, even if the majority of the ecclesiastical centres established in the seventh and eighth centuries were disrupted, many of them can still be traced in fragments of sculpture and in surviving church fabric. Above all, in the Venerable Bede Northumbria could boast one of the great intellectual and religious figures of Europe.

TWO

SPIRITUALITY AND THE MODERN CHURCH

C H R I S T O P H E R   L E W I S

NO PART OF ENGLAND IS MORE STEEPED IN SPIRITUALITY THAN NORTHUMBERLAND

Our story begins with a battle. In 633, Oswald, son of a previous (English/Angle) king of Northumbria, set up a wooden cross on a battlefield, and after bidding his troops to pray went on to defeat the (Celtic) king Caedwalla of Gwynedd at Heavenfield. The church of St Oswald stands on the presumed site of the battle, and an annual pilgrimage to it takes place on the nearest Saturday to 5 August, St Oswald's Day, following the route taken centuries ago by monks from Hexham Abbey.

Oswald had been converted to Christianity by the (Celtic) monks of Iona, so it was to these he turned to assist in instructing the people of Northumbria in the new faith. Aidan was sent, and in 635 he came to Lindisfarne. Ever since, Holy Island has been a focus of pilgrimage. The resurgence of interest in Celtic spirituality means that this is as strong today as it ever has been.

Many people attracted to this spirituality have a romantic, rather naïve picture of what it entailed. They enjoy pictures of St Cuthbert with the seals and other local fauna – a precursor of St Francis (whose twenty-first-century brothers have their much-visited friary down the coast at Alnmouth). What many may not realise is that the otters that also appear in these pictures came to lie on his feet to warm them up, after he had spent all night standing waist-deep in the sea, reciting the Psalms. Many miles away and nearly a century earlier, St David had been called the 'water man', probably for the same reason. They were tough people, those Celts.

Cuthbert moved from Lindisfarne to spend the last years of his life as a hermit on Inner Farne, and many today visit this island on boat trips from Seahouses. After he died, in 687, his body was brought to Lindisfarne for burial. It was not allowed to rest in peace. Threat of Viking invasion caused the monks to dig him up. He was passed from pillar to post, often in hiding, until eventually finding a permanent tomb in Durham Cathedral 300 years later. The magnificent *Lindisfarne Gospels* (now in the British Museum) went on the journey with his coffin. The church of St Mary the Virgin on Holy Island currently hosts Fenwick Lawson's superb carving *The Journey*. Slightly larger than life-size, carved in elm, it depicts three pairs of monks carrying St Cuthbert's coffin. It suggests movement, grim determination, oppression.

It was not only the Vikings who oppressed the Church of the day; there was also division between the different traditions of the Celtic and the Roman Churches. At the Synod of Whitby in 664, one of those who helped swing the argument in the direction of Rome was

St Wilfrid, who was to found Hexham Abbey in 674. The history is ancient, but its echoes can be discerned not only in the places of today but also in today's thirst for spirituality.

THE MODERN CHURCH IS OFTEN BETTER AT RELIGION THAN AT SPIRITUALITY

In English, the words 'religion' and 'spirituality' hide their meaning. Dig into their origins, however, and you find some interesting suggestions.

'Spirituality' comes from the Latin *spiro*, meaning 'I breathe'. The same link between 'spirit' and 'breath' is also there in the Hebrew and Greek of the Bible; indeed the Hebrew word, *ruach*, is thought to imitate the sound of the wind. So 'spirituality' is speaking about an experience that can be felt, that moves us, that 'blows where it chooses', as Jesus says to Nicodemus. Like the wind, it is difficult to capture and impossible to control.

'Religion', on the other hand, comes from a Latin word meaning to 'tie down'. It is an attempt to 'tie down' the experience of the spirit. This can be helpful. Religion gives us a language in which to articulate experience that is beyond words. It provides contexts – buildings, liturgy, music, art – in which the experience of the spiritual can be shared and even generated. The Bible tells of living experiences of God's presence with his people, but he or she is a God who cannot be tied down by human manipulation, as Moses learnt at the burning bush: 'I am who I am' is an assurance of active presence, not a name that can conjure up a genie to be used at will. Yet the catechism of the *Book of Common Prayer* suggests that in sacraments God does choose voluntarily to tie himself down. Many people know its definition of a sacrament as the 'outward and visible sign of an inward and spiritual grace'; fewer remember that it continues with 'a means whereby we receive [that grace], and a pledge to assure us thereof'. Jesus himself can be described as the sacrament of God: the creative spirit tied to human flesh.

Religion becomes unhelpful when the spirit is overtaken by the tying-down, when dogma is more important than experience, when forms of worship take precedence over content, when rules are more important than an encounter with a God who loves. The conflict between Jesus and the religious leaders of the day arises in part at least from this having happened. It has often happened in the Church, too, where authority and control – tying-down – have taken precedence over individuals' experience of God. William Tyndale was burnt at the stake for translating the Bible into language that people could understand. The Church of England's suspicion of 'enthusiasm' in the eighteenth century – defined by Samuel Johnson as 'a vain confidence of Divine favour or communication' – was one of the reasons for the rise of Methodism as a separate Church. The anxiety in some parts of the Roman Catholic Church at the appointment of Cardinal Ratzinger as Pope Benedict XVI bubbled over in a hard-hitting editorial in *The Tablet* at the end of October 2005, when the conservative outcome of the International Synod of Bishops gave rise to the comment: 'There are clearly outstanding pastors among the bishops of the Church, but for too long and too often safe but second-rate men have also been promoted: men whose mediocrity caused them to be perceived as safe by control-minded Curial officials'.

It is hardly surprising that today, when so much authority is questioned, and the mood of thinking described as 'post-modernism' allows each person's experience to be as valid as the next, many have turned away from religion. 'Spirituality' is welcomed all over the place, but religion, the tying-down of this experience, is often dismissed as so much old rope; and the Church is perceived as being about religion, not spirituality.

Interestingly, spirituality is seen as important in areas of secular life. As far back as the 1944 Education Act there was mention of children's spiritual needs. This was reaffirmed by the 1988 Education Reform Act, which requires a school's spiritual, moral, social and cultural aspects to be inspected. In 1992 the (UK) National Health Service Management Executive published guidelines on 'Meeting the Spiritual Needs of Patients and Staff'. The Charter of Fundamental Rights for Europe, adopted by the European Council in Biarritz in 2000, spoke of Europe's 'spiritual and moral heritage'. In at least the first and last of these examples, it is instructive that the word 'spiritual' is to some extent a way of avoiding using the more controversial 'religious'.

One of the clearest explorations of how widespread spirituality is, but also of how negatively the Church is perceived, can be seen in a report on research undertaken by David Hay and Kate Hunt of the Centre for the Study of Human Relations at the University of Nottingham.[1]

The authors quote research suggesting 'that slightly more than 76 per cent of the national population are now likely to admit to having had a spiritual or religious experience'. Examples they give of such experience are: a patterning of events, awareness of the presence of God, awareness of prayer being answered, awareness of a sacred presence in nature, awareness of the presence of the dead, and awareness of an evil presence.[2] Elsewhere they speak of the commonest response to their own research conversations as being 'a conviction that there is 'something there".[3]

They add the comment, however, that 'the great majority of these people are of course not regular churchgoers'. They also write: 'In general we found that people were to varying degrees defensive at the beginning of the conversations, and then gradually relaxed as they realized that we did not have a hidden agenda either to criticise or to convert them, and that we were genuinely interested in their own views'.[4]

One of the case studies they describe in detail is 'Matthew'.

> [He] feels very strongly that religious people in general are arrogant in their assumption that they are the bearers of the truth … For Matthew, and many other people we spoke with, belonging to the institutional Church means that you have to believe with certainty, there is no room for doubt. But this is just not possible for him as he reflects on his own life and the world around him. Matthew's spirituality is dynamic, it changes with his life; there is no room for a once-and-for-all revelation. Yet he gives the impression of longing to be able to belong to a faith community, a place where he can explore his beliefs and develop his spirituality.[5]

A further sign of this longing to explore spirituality is the plethora of television programmes that have taken place since that report was published. Examples are: *Battle for the Soul of Britain*, *Spirituality Shopper* (introduced by local man Jonathan Edwards) and Jonathan Miller's *A History of Disbelief*. The series *Monastery* concluded with a remarkable scene where silence was held seemingly for many minutes while a participant opened himself to the spiritual impact of what he had experienced. *A Country Parish* and *A Seaside Parish* have both been influential in driving TV programmers' perception of what interests an audience of largely non-churchgoing but nevertheless spiritually aware people.

There are signs that the Church is alert to the need to allow spirituality to flourish, and for religion to be a benign force, though there are also contrary signs.

The publication of the various rites comprising *Common Worship* is one such benign sign. The Preface to *Services and Prayers* is clear about the importance of tying us together: 'The forms of worship authorized in the Church of England express our faith and help to create our identity'.[6] This is religion as it should be. At the same time there is a freedom about the *Common Worship* services, a freedom to quarry whatever is appropriate for any group of people. 'The services provided here are rich and varied ….They encourage an imaginative engagement in worship, opening the way for people in the varied circumstances of their lives to experience the love of God in Jesus Christ in the life and power of the Holy Spirit'.[7] What more appropriate description of spirituality in the context of worship could there be? *Common Worship* is, of course, only a quarry. It places great responsibility on those who plan and conduct worship, as well as on congregations, to be open to a degree of novelty and experimentation.

This is not to say that only innovative worship feeds spirituality. There remain many who are fed by the *Book of Common Prayer*, as well as by traditional art and music. The rise in the popularity of icons, particularly of Rublev's *Trinity*, and the impact of Rembrandt's *Prodigal Son*, not least as a result of Henri Nouwen's book *Return of the Prodigal Son*,[8] illustrates this.

As far as traditional music is concerned, John V. Taylor in his book *The Christlike God* quotes somebody who had listened to Bach's *B minor Mass* in Ely Cathedral and had found it an encounter with the 'numinous' that was positively frightening.[9] I can still remember the impact, when a boy chorister, of singing Fauré's *Requiem* in King's Chapel in Cambridge on All Souls' Day. The celebrant wore black vestments, and in the dimness of the candle-lit chapel the only times he could be seen appeared to be when he raised his hands or turned his face to the congregation. The sense of mystery was profound. More recently, millions were moved by John Tavener's *Song for Athene* at Princess Diana's funeral. And how many times has Classic FM been asked to play Arvo Pärt's *Spiegel im Spiegel*? How often has it been used in churches and retreat houses in meditations?

A further sign of spirituality flourishing in worship is the widespread appeal of the music of Taizé and Iona. In each case the spirituality, in terms of the inner experience of God's presence in the worship, is closely linked to an awareness of God's demand for justice and peace. This is a reminder that the publication of *Faith in the City* in 1985,[10] and all the concern for deprived communities both in inner cities and in rural areas ever since, is as much a part of the way God's wind blows his Church as what goes on inside the church buildings. Indeed, here too religion and spirituality go hand in hand. A secular emphasis on spirituality can often seem to be self-centred indulgence. It is the common commitment within a church community that enables members of a diocese to support each other in costly living and action. Examples of this happening in the Newcastle Diocese can be found in the inner city of Newcastle itself.

The *Urban Ministry and Theology Project* has redistributed clergy responsibilities across the four churches of Byker in such a way as to enable partnerships with other bodies to be created that involve a degree of sharing of ownership of both property and agenda that is, for the Church, highly unusual. One of the church buildings, St Michael's, was in such a state that the congregation has been worshipping in a shop; something described as 'scary, then exciting'. All this challenges conventional expectations of where spirituality is to be found.

Breathing Space is a forum jointly run by the chaplaincy at Northumbria University with a group of people who wanted permission to 'think the unthinkable'. It arranges about four events a year with speakers from a variety of traditions. A 'Matthew' could certainly feel at home here.

Places can be as spiritually creative today as they have ever been. Our broader spiritual life is served by public sculpture such as the *Angel of the North* or the building of the Sage Music Centre. Where is the Church sponsoring art? (This is a question, not an implied suggestion that it is not doing so!) Where are church buildings kept open and presented as vehicles for spiritual exploration?

St Oswald's, Heavenfield, with which this chapter began, is always open, and, appropriately, is reached by crossing a field. It is beautifully kept, clean and with fresh flowers, and has attractive information boards at the west end, but it is devoid of music or welcomers, standing silent on its windy ridge yards from the line of Hadrian's Wall, attracting visitors from all over the world, feeding their imagination. Hexham Abbey is understandably much more busy, though mercifully free of the hordes of tourists of, say, a Canterbury Cathedral, which only really comes alive when the place is locked up for the night. Hexham draws attention to its past with its signage, and its offer of votive candles and the opportunity for silent prayer in St Wilfrid's chapel is popular. In the parish church at Edlingham a booklet is available to passing tourists that encourages them to explore the various parts of the building as sacred space, and to move from exploring to praying.

Nowhere in the diocese is more of a centre of pilgrimage than Holy Island. St Mary's attempts to meet people in whatever spiritual frame of mind they come. Sometimes it has recorded music playing. Always there are votive candles on offer. A variety of prayer cards is available. Some are appropriate for those who come on an explicitly Christian pilgrimage, many at the end of a five-day walk along St Cuthbert's Way from Melrose. Another card offers a sceptic's prayer. There is also a welcome card, taking the opportunity presented by people coming into the church for whatever motive to tell of the Christian faith in this place known as a cradle of Christianity.

Of course church buildings are not the only 'places' the Church has to offer. In an age of hunger for spirituality but reluctance to commit to the Church, retreat houses around the country are a particularly valuable resource, as they are less obviously part of the 'institution'. Shepherds Dene, which was gifted to the Bishop of Newcastle as a retreat house in 1946, is an example of this. It is used not only by groups from churches but also by many secular bodies. A significant attraction is the atmosphere. A former Area Development Officer for the National Association of Citizens' Advice Bureaux commented about bringing her staff to Shepherds Dene for training days: 'When we came to Shepherds Dene, there were no ragged tempers about as there sometimes were elsewhere, people were much more relaxed, and the days were much more productive. The peacefulness put everybody in a right state of mind for a day's training.' Similarly, a member of a group of University staff members said of a recent meeting there: 'We felt as if we had come into a different world'.

In order to build on this, in 2002 a group of volunteers constructed a replica of the labyrinth that had been built into the floor of Chartres Cathedral in about 1220. This was seen as an opportunity to offer a tool for spiritual exploration that might be used by people who had come with either religious or quite secular intent. Even before it was finished, that vision was being realised. Somebody who was running a training event in the house for an NHS trust saw what the volunteers were doing, and the next day came with her wellies in order to help with the work. She has since brought other groups to use the labyrinth, and there are many comments in the scrapbook in the house which show how widely it has been appreciated.

So, worship, art, music, place are all ways in which the Church makes opportunities which allow spirituality to flourish. Perhaps the greatest ambiguity arises when it comes to the Church's use of the Bible. I have often seen people light up as the insights of biblical criticism have allowed the experience of the men and women of past ages to come alive, and to reflect and inform their own glimpses of wonder or anger, despair or amazement. Yet so often the Church is seen to use the Bible primarily as a source of proof texts with which to attack those whose views differ from their own. The Church may claim to have 'good news', but its own behaviour can seem to be very bad news indeed.

The Chinese ideogram for 'crisis' consists of two characters: 'danger' and 'opportunity'. We are not short of people suggesting the Church faces a crisis, partly caused by the diminishing numbers of those who attend worship and contribute financially. The 'danger' is illustrated by Hay and Hunt. They comment: 'cynicism about the religious institution … is the 'default mode' in public discourse, as was made very clear in the focus groups when people were asked for their opinion of the Church'.[11]

The 'opportunity' is presented by the widespread thirst for spirituality. To some extent the Church is taking this opportunity, but only to some extent, and usually within the walls of the Church. To take seriously the Spirit who 'blows where it chooses', we need to be humble, to listen, to offer to help interpret people's experience that takes place beyond the boundaries of 'church'. 'Our role is to be listeners' suggest Hay and Hunt in their final chapter, 'Reflections on Mission'. 'Ideally what we discover together is a non-oppressive, mutually respectful mode of dialogue across the cultural divide that increasingly separates the secular and religious worlds ….We suggest that the development of this dialogue is the work of mission.'[12]

The Church in our diocese has a wonderful spiritual history, from Heavenfield to Holy Island. It would be good if we could say that engaging with twenty-first century people's spirituality is like taking coals to Newcastle.

THREE

SEARCHING FOR IDENTITY: THE SOCIAL, ECONOMIC AND CULTURAL CONTEXT OF NEWCASTLE DIOCESE

PETER ROBINSON

In its 125th anniversary the communities of Newcastle Diocese are increasingly complex and fragile, full of potential yet also of uncertainty, eager to reposition themselves within a rapidly changing economic environment, and with doubts about what this might mean.

The Church has aligned itself with the growth of the voluntary sector and is involved in local regeneration programmes such as New Deal for Communities, the Ouseburn Trust and the Walker Riverside Partnership Board. Some parishes have entered neighbourhood partnerships with statutory agencies, voluntary groups and community organisations around specific themes – for example at Byker, St Martin in working with children and their families and at Byker, St Silas tackling the issue of homelessness.

Many parishes are reordering their buildings as resources to allow new alliances to come into being through a much wider community use – among others, recent work at Gunnerton, St Christopher, Stannington, St Mary, Percy Main, St John, Fawdon, St Mary, and Scotswood, St Margaret illustrates this creative involvement. Other parishes such as Longbenton, St Mary, Denton, Holy Spirit and the Benwell Team are discovering partnership through their involvement with community youth work. The Church Urban Fund has provided over £2 million worth of grants and a local scheme will continue this momentum. Sharing responsibility for the future of society in partnership with others has many implications for the local identity of the Church and for its patterns of ministry.

THE SOCIAL, ECONOMIC AND CULTURAL CONTEXT OF THE DIOCESE

Newcastle upon Tyne is the centre of gravity of north-east England. Its reputation as 'party city' attracts many to the 'noise, banter, affability and exuberant sense of social ownership of [its] central area'.[1] The city's ambition to be world-class in higher education, tourism and culture and creative industries, its desire to be a national leader in retailing, financial and health services, symbolise the need for the region to position itself within a global, informational economy.[2] But compared with other regions in the United Kingdom the economic performance of the North-East is weak. Indicators of innovation such as self-employment, qualification levels and expenditure on research and development by local businesses are all below average.[3]

The diocese is often said to be 'a rural diocese with an urban fringe', with its urban areas in the south-east, influenced by the legacy of the coalfields. It includes Alnwick, the market town voted 'Best place in Britain to live' by *Country Life* magazine in 2002, but it also has some of the highest levels of deprivation in the United Kingdom.

This chapter focuses on the social, economic and cultural factors which characterise the context of the diocese and which shed light on the region's search for a fulfilling and sustainable identity.

REINVENTION OF NEWCASTLE

Newcastle is in transition. Its traditional industrial infrastructure is gone. Amidst the gloomy prospect of a gradually declining population, the city council launched a major programme for regeneration in June 2000: *Going for Growth*. This offered a vision for a competitive, cohesive and cosmopolitan city.

Going for Growth highlights important themes for many communities in the diocese. First of all, there is a need to reinvent the social and economic basis of the region. Many community leaders recognise that in order to thrive in the future Newcastle has to align itself with the underlying movements of the global economy and face dramatic change. Secondly, there is a need for partnership. Mistakes in the consultation process of *Going for Growth* revealed a deep-rooted assumption by the 'City Fathers' that they could ignore the wishes and wisdom of grassroots communities. Thirdly, there are questions about the role of the community and voluntary sector. *Going for Growth* wrongly suggested that community processes were of little value and not robust enough to help address present needs.

FOOT-AND-MOUTH DISEASE IN NORTHUMBERLAND

On 23 February 2001 an outbreak of Foot-and-Mouth Disease began in Northumberland – and devastated the countryside. Three hundred farms in Northumberland suffered a livestock cull; nearly a quarter of a million animals were slaughtered. The tourism industry in Northumberland was hit as rights of way were closed and visitors were encouraged to stay away. Ugly, environmentally detrimental, funeral pyres dominated the television news for weeks. The public inquiry launched by Northumberland County Council highlighted the emotional impact of the crisis caused by the long period of isolation for the county – Northumberland was the last county in England to be deemed free of the disease in November 2001 – and also by the long-term health implications for its inhabitants, especially children.[4]

Like *Going for Growth* in Newcastle, the impact of Foot-and-Mouth Disease in Northumberland highlighted key themes for the communities of the diocese. Many in the farming community were compelled to adopt alternative employment. Tourism was re-emphasised as a significant part of the rural economy. But many city-dwellers did not appreciate the deeper impact of Foot-and-Mouth Disease on underlying issues of food consumption, the dominance of supermarket consumerism and consequent pressures on the agricultural sector to farm more intensively. The rural and the urban were often seen as unrelated and distinct, but the experience of 2001 highlighted the importance of a 'city region' – the concept that cities have permeable boundaries and that the relationship between town and countryside is one of mutual dependence. Questions to do with the environment could no longer be seen as an exclusively rural issue.

SEARCHING FOR IDENTITY

Across the North-East there is a search for new ways of being, for new and sustainable economic patterns, for new links with other parts of the United Kingdom, Europe and beyond. Individuals, communities and the voluntary sector are looking to find new ways of cooperation. People are adapting to an economy that requires greater innovation and a wider skills base; they are seeking a new understanding of the interrelatedness of the disparate parts of the region's life and are becoming more aware of environmental issues.

Five themes illustrate the development in the region's identity in the early twenty-first century – increasing ethnic diversity, changing structures of local governance, the growth of partnerships, the nuances of regeneration and the importance of tourism and culture.

1 Ethnic and social diversity

The North-East has a reputation for being predominantly ethnically white although the extent and impact of Irish and Scottish immigration during the nineteenth century are often overlooked, as is the migration of local people away from the city.[5] There are some well-known exceptions: the west end of Newcastle experienced immigration from the Commonwealth in the post-war period, South Shields has hosted a Yemeni Arab community since the late nineteenth century and Gateshead is home to an orthodox Jewish community.

Within the diocese there are some small but significant trends. In North Tyneside, where the numbers of the Pakistani, Bangladeshi, Indian, Chinese and Afro-Caribbean communities are small, significant communities are only now beginning to form.[6]

In Newcastle the major minority ethnic communities are Pakistani, Bangladeshi, Indian, Chinese and Afro-Caribbean. Between 1991 and 2001 the minority ethnic population increased from 4.1-6.9 per cent of the total population. Those of ethnic origin in South Asia increased from 2.9-4.1 per cent. There are other significant groups not revealed by the statistics: for example, an increasing number of people from eastern Europe. In 2000 there was also a significant increase in asylum-seekers settling in Newcastle. There is anecdotal evidence that some Newcastle communities now host over 30 language groups.

The voluntary sector has led the way in supporting incomers, making practical efforts towards integration and enabling struggling communities to recognise new energy and talents. Alongside the statutory agencies and regional charitable organisations such as the North of England Refugee Service community groups have been the most effective local agencies, supported by many Church leaders.[7] The work of The Black and Ethnic Community Organisations Network (BECON) is also notable, as it challenges the social exclusion of minority ethnic communities, provides training opportunities and facilitates the networking of black and minority ethnic groups.

There is also greater religious diversity. The growth of religious pluralism in the North-East, particularly on Tyneside, led to the establishment of Newcastle's Council of Faiths in 2005. This is a bold sign that a new configuration of religious groupings is required. It signalled a willingness by the major faith groups to work together on common issues and requires the churches to see interfaith dialogue in a new framework of action focused on the regeneration of local communities. It values the perspectives of faith groups who experience North-Eastern life quite differently from more established communities.

The Tyneside novelist, the late Julia Darling, pointed out that communities in the North-East already have the inner resources to embrace what she called 'cosmopolitanism': that is 'we could only be truly cosmopolitan if we studied the place where we lived, our family histories and the stories of our past'.[8] If the diverse elements that have traditionally made up local life in the North-East can be treasured, then we have a resource through which to embrace relationships with people who have very different ethnic origins. The way forward offers a discovery of a regional culture that is much more varied, diverse and dynamic than the traditional stereotypes suggest. The growth of local studies, for example, is another important step in this direction.[9]

2 Local governance

One feature of the North-East, as in other regions, has been the growing complexity of local governance, especially during the past decade. In 1999 central government established the North-East Assembly. A representative rather than elected body, it represents the region to central government. It holds the regional development agency 'One NorthEast' financially accountable, which in turn is responsible for a Regional Economic Strategy. Other government agencies focus on specific areas of work including, for example, Arts Council England, North-East. Alongside such agencies a Government Office North-East represents central government and its policies.

Although these layers of regional governance have developed, there is a democratic deficit in many communities. In some urban areas the turnout in local elections has fallen well below 15 per cent. Many thought that the referendum in the autumn of 2004 to create a Directly Elected Regional Assembly would herald a rejuvenation of the electoral process, but the resounding 'No' vote suggested that the decline in involvement would continue. This rejection was, perhaps, understandable in that the proposals did not appear to offer substantial delegated decision-making. As the Bishop of Newcastle remarked in the House of Lords a few days after the referendum, 'if the people in the North-East had felt that they had been given a real opportunity to exercise some real power to shape their own destiny, the vote might well have been very different'.[10]

Recent research in some of the region's most deprived communities suggests that whilst families and whole communities continue to have low living standards, limited opportunities for personal and community development and insufficient access to key facilities, they are more interested in survival than in getting involved in politics.[11]

3 Partnership

It is widely accepted, however, that local people need to be involved in finding solutions to local problems if these are to be successful and sustainable. The key to good partnership goes beyond the demands of government policy to an acknowledgement that no one organisation has all the answers.

Formal partnerships have grown across the diocese during the last decade. Each local authority now has a Local Strategic Partnership. The Newcastle Partnership, committed to 'a new way of getting better services for local people',[12] is responsible for the delivery of central government's Neighbourhood Renewal National Strategy Action Plan and also, as one of the most deprived local authority areas in England, for apportioning a Neighbourhood Renewal Fund. The Northumberland Strategic Partnership seeks to promote the bold vision that by 2010 Northumberland is 'well connected and proud of its people, heritage, excellence and ambition'.[13] North Tyneside's Strategic Partnership embodies its values and hopes for the communities of the borough in a 'Shared Plan'. Top of the list is the desire to 'increase opportunities for people to be listened to, to make a difference and to be kept informed'.[14] Many neighbourhood partnerships also take a substantial level of responsibility (including funding) for improving difficult areas.

The concept of partnership itself is a significant development in a region that has not always sought to involve local people in determining the shape of their social, economic and cultural environment. If some communites have been used to the guaranteed provision of employment, housing and other services by dominant institutions, then living in an era when those institutions can no longer provide for them is a real challenge.

Partnership requires new styles of working. Elected members no longer act simply as providers for dependent communities but now must enable communities to articulate realistic hopes. Equally, local residents need to be encouraged to take appropriate responsibility for the future rather than rely on the traditional providers. Recent research asks the poignant question: can the distribution of power be negotiated in such a way that effective trust is established between grass roots communities and agencies that in the past have acted in a well-meaning but top-down fashion?[15]

Partnership, therefore, represents something of a renaissance of participative democracy, but challenges remain: to make the language of governance intelligible, to empower local people in working with well-resourced personnel from statutory agencies, and to catalyse a truly creative contribution from local communities rather than burden them with a disproportionate workload.

4 Regeneration

David Byrne shows that the region became more industrial than it had ever been in 1970. Although the collapse of the mining industry from the heights of the early 1920s was substantial, this was more than offset by two positive changes: growing opportunities for women in work from the 1930s and successful male redeployment in new manufacturing industries in the 1960s.[16] However, by the turn of the millennium the effects of globalisation had become unavoidable as the nineteenth- and twentieth-century industries had all but been eliminated and manufacturing accounted for less than 15 per cent of all employment. Commerce, leisure and retailing seem to be leading the way to an economy based on consumption rather than production.[17] The region needs to be 'rescued from the stigma of industrial decline'.

Regeneration seeks to look at the renewal of the whole of society, but those societies which live within an outdated industrial framework have little chance of relating effectively to the world today. Questions to do with education, housing, the nature of communities and access to services are crucial; but the sharpness of economic realities and the requirement for the North-East to compete mean that communities are sometimes excluded from the heart of the practice of regeneration.

There are, however, also good examples of people taking responsibility for their own futures. This is the case in Northumberland, where the low density of population across the county presents a particular challenge.[18] Northumberland Community Council, an umbrella body for the voluntary sector, has been influential in the development of a wider range of voluntary and community organisations. It has supported the growth of a number of Development Trusts in places such as Amble, Belford, North Sunderland and Seahouses and Alnwick. These aspire to lead the task of regeneration by shaping their locality's infrastructure and residents' involvement, so that confidence and participation can be improved to achieve economic prosperity. Another example is the Rural Voices Network, which uses information technology to improve communication between members of the farming community, voluntary groups, business people and the public sector.[19]

5 Culture and tourism

Culture and tourism are central to both the future economy and pride of the North-East.[20] The focus for the cultural agenda was the 2002 Newcastle-Gateshead bid to become European Capital of Culture in 2008. Although unsuccessful, it was a vehicle for debating the place of culture within the life of the region and gave birth to 'Culture[10]' ('Culture to the power of 10'), a decade of high-profile events, an early example of which was the hosting of the Tall Ships race in 2005. The Regional Cultural Strategy for the North-East of England, drawn up by the consortium Culture North-East, builds on the distinctive character of the people and the place, and promotes competition with other regions nationally and throughout Europe. A number of music festivals – for example, in Rothbury, Berwick-upon-Tweed, at the Mouth of the Tyne, Orange Evolution on the Newcastle-Gateshead Quayside and in Alnwick – are designed to attract new visitors and promote the image of the region. Sporting events such as the Great North Run, now one of the most popular half-marathons in Europe, and the marketing of the region's leading football teams are other important ingredients.

Tourism already supports around 10 per cent of jobs in the region. There are precise targets for the growth of tourists – and for their spending on each visit. But the North-East is still the least visited region in the country. The rural and coastal areas of Northumberland – now branded 'the Blue Sky County' – are one focus: Alnwick Castle and the Gardens, for example, seek to attract international visitors, as does the United Nations Educational, Scientific and Cultural Organisation (UNESCO) World Heritage site of Hadrian's Wall. The farming community is finding a fresh use for redundant farm buildings to provide tourist accommodation, and, through farm shops, to sell local foodstuffs and local arts and crafts products. It uses the internet to build on the Northumberland brand.

However, this emphasis on culture and tourism brings new tensions. One lies between an understanding of culture as the lived expression of local values and beliefs and an understanding of the arts and performance as located within significant institutions. For me, this is embodied by the view from Newcastle's east quayside – now dominated by the Sage Music Centre, the Baltic Centre for Contemporary Art, the Gateshead Millennium Bridge and highly priced riverside apartments – into the community of Byker, clearly visible because of its distinctive architecture (the 'Byker Wall' – which represents contemporary disadvantage), which also has its own vibrant cultural heritage reaching back to the industrial revolution.

Another tension is between culture as a new industrial base for the region and culture as art. Cultural regeneration brings new jobs but also worries that this reduces culture to a commodity within a consumerist worldview, which potentially devalues and compromises the distinctiveness of the region's contribution to a national cultural project.[21]

There is one other important factor: many locals believe that Northumberland is one of the nation's best kept secrets: 'Shhh! Don't tell anyone!' Whilst the economic benefits of high-profile cultural and tourism strategies are urgently sought, negotiation continues between the demands that a global economy makes on a small region within a growing European Union and an internal desire for a more insular existence.

THE IMPLICATIONS FOR THE CHURCH

Each of these five areas impacts on the life of its parish churches in the diocese. Recent research highlights the contribution that faith groups make to the development of human relationships and the social networks that enable whole communities to flourish.[22] This contribution has sometimes been overlooked, not least by churches themselves, and more thought is required to see how parishes might make best use of their resources to serve their localities and help take responsibility for determining appropriate patterns of community life.

One theme for regeneration is that of vision. In 2005 the Bishop of Newcastle held a series of consultations asking 'what would make Newcastle a good city?' Some results of an event for young people were reported in a national report *Faithful Cities*.[23] The findings have the potential to inform a wider debate, not just about developing a realistic vision in itself but also about how that vision might be brought into being.

The region's Christian heritage is itself a rich resource for tourism and culture. The church on Holy Island and at Hexham clearly has a central part to play, but other initiatives are being taken – for example, in the Hexham deanery through information leaflets on local churches, in the north-east of the diocese with a publication 'In the Steps of the Saints' and with plans in Wooler to develop a staging-post on St Cuthbert's Way. Important steps forward include creative uses of information technology and a greater integration of the Celtic spiritual tradition within the region's strategies for renewal, the schools of the diocese and the life of the churches.

As the North-East region continues to search for its new identity, the local church is called to join in and play its own distinctive part. It does this recognising that it too will be reformed in the process. Newcastle Diocese for the majority of its 125 years has been a symbol of the Church's commitment to the lives of those who were engaged in the project of the industrial revolution. Today, it is important that the diocese continues to be a symbol of the Church's commitment to finding the love of God in the processes of change required for the development of sustainable communities. Perhaps the greatest contribution that could be made is for the Church to live within the tensions this chapter has identified, to be a travelling companion with a region that is searching for its new role and to ensure that the voices of the weakest within its boundaries are given a dignified hearing.

FOUR

THE CHURCH IN THE CITY

CHRISTOPHER DALLISTON

INTRODUCTION

Newcastle-Gateshead is full of striking new landmark structures. Standing on the terrace of one of these, the new Sage Concert Hall, you can look down the river to the revamped Baltic flour-mill, now an exhibition space for contemporary art, and itself a symbol of the city's transition from commerce to culture; across the river to St James's Park, which commands both the horizon and the hearts and hopes of thousands of Geordies; and along the river at the Millennium Bridge, the latest in a sequence of bridges which have collectively become, perhaps, the city's unique trademark. You will also be able to admire the redeveloped Quayside, where sheds and warehouses have been replaced by the lawcourts, offices, hotels, restaurants and bars, while dotted across the cityscape are the less successful reminders of previous attempts at renewal: the glass and concrete blocks that characterised the hubris of the 1970s.

For all the efforts of the recent and not so recent past, however, it is still the churches, their towers and spires punctuating the skyline, that are among the most distinguished and distinctive features of Newcastle's panorama.

The slender spire of Pugin's Roman Catholic Cathedral of St Mary, the elegant eighteenth-century tower and spire of All Saints and the extraordinary medieval crown lantern of St Nicholas Cathedral rise above the city's river frontage while, to the west, the blackened tower of St Matthew looks down on the city centre. To the east the church of St Ann can be glimpsed (at least for the present), apparently perched on the slope overlooking the river.

Not all the city's churches and certainly not all their treasures are revealed from this vantage point. Cross the river and pass the cathedral on the way to Central Station and you will encounter St John the Baptist's, believed to date from the mid-twelfth century. A little to the north you will pass St Andrew, which like so many of Newcastle's churches is almost hidden within its commercial surroundings but once revealed shows a building which retains a significant amount of its Romanesque character. It claims to be the oldest extant ecclesiastical building in the city. Finally, continue to the Haymarket and St Thomas's stands proudly, if a little starkly, as the focal point of this busy crossroads with the City Hall as a backdrop, flanked by the city's two Universities (of Newcastle and Northumbria). Add to these landmark buildings Brunswick Methodist Chapel and St James's United Reformed Church (among others) and it is clear that Newcastle's churches offer a very significant dimension to its landscape.

The churches of Newcastle are not, however, monuments to past glories but continue to play an active part in the life of the city. Each offers its own unique contribution to that task.

Tradition, resources, location, and the vision of the particular communities are all helping to shape its work and mission for the future.

SOME CHARACTERISTICS OF CITY CENTRE MINISTRY

Before we can adequately explore the contribution of particular churches it is worth making some general observations about what 'being a church' means in the city, and to note some of the differences from traditional patterns of ministry in the suburbs or the countryside. While new models are being explored everywhere, it is clear that, in the city, churches have long been in the vanguard of such thinking.

Who?

It is clear that whilst there has been some renewed growth in the numbers of city centre residents in recent years, it remains the case that the churches do not serve a stable residential community but draw their membership from far and wide. They have congregations that are very largely eclectic in character. Indeed, for the most part, even the clergy live outside the boundaries of the parish. While this is not unique to city centre ministry (especially in an increasingly mobile society), it means that the city centre parishes draw their local character less from those who choose to worship there than from the context in which they are set. Indeed the mission of individual churches often has a clear emphasis on making strong connections to people who work locally or have some other investment in the city centre. In any eclectic situation this has the potential for tension over 'ownership' between the congregation and between those whose primary focus is the locality. It is a mark, perhaps, of the distinctive character of each of the churches that this does not seem to be the case in Newcastle.

Where?

While location has some bearing on the roles of the various churches, parish boundaries have almost no meaning in the city centre. Ministry tends to be issue and network-based rather than geographically-focussed. Again, while this is perhaps an increasingly common feature of post-modern or 'fresh' expressions of 'church', it is a marked feature of the city centre. Parochial boundaries are significant in the conduct of occasional offices (baptisms, weddings and funerals), but these form a relatively modest part of city centre ministry. In 2005 the four Anglican city churches together celebrated just twelve baptisms, four funerals and eight weddings. None of these were on behalf of individuals resident in the city centre. About half were for individuals or families with a long-term relationship with a particular church; the rest involved people who had connections to a church through institutions with which the church had a particular relationship or partnership.

When?

A third distinctive feature of city centre ministry is that it is not exclusively or even primarily Sunday-based. All four Anglican churches are engaged in a seven-day-a-week ministry. At St John and the Cathedral, the Daily Offices and a daily celebration of the Eucharist are important dimensions in the rhythm of prayer. Other special services also form an important dimension of the ministry of all four churches. The cathedral refectory welcomes visitors from Monday to Friday; at St Thomas a fair trade shop is open throughout the week. St Andrew opens its Hall as a drop-in for homeless people and drug users. The city centre churches serve as role models to churches elsewhere that are trying to develop patterns of ministry and uses for their buildings that are more flexible and more responsive to the times that people are able to use them.

Ministry in context

The task of the city centre churches is to respond to events, networks and issues. This is both creative and challenging, demanding flexibility but also requiring the churches to articulate their particular sense of mission and identity if there is not to be an unhelpful sense of competitiveness and duplication.

Different personalities bring different gifts and the wider culture constantly shifts. Indeed the city's own focus has shifted over the past decades. The relocation of the city's administrative hub to the present Civic Centre and the post-war decline of the river frontage saw the city move up the hill, only for the regeneration of the Quayside and Grainger Town to draw the focus back towards the river again.

Against that background the churches have sought to shape their priorities. St Thomas has a particular concern for issues of justice and world development. It has established something of a campaigning role in areas such as debt relief and fair trade, summed up by the statement etched on the glass doors of the church: 'Hate Evil, Love Good, Do Justice at the Gate'.

St Andrew, close to Eldon Square Shopping Centre, acts as the base for the City Centre Chaplaincy. Over 30 years it has established its credentials as a place that explores and speaks out on issues to do with the commercial life of the city; on work but also on worklessness, seeking not only to offer pastoral care but also a prophetic dimension to its witness.

St John, close to Central Station and *en route* to the Monument, makes a virtue of its crossroads location. It operates an open door policy, building on its traditional role as a place of prayer and worship, and acting as a haven of stillness amid the busyness all around. This offers numerous opportunities for a ministry of counselling and of pastoral care.

The cathedral is defined by its statutes as 'the seat of the bishop and a centre of worship and mission'. Much flows from that in terms of diocesan services and events and in its tradition of choral excellence. But context remains important, and St Nicholas has sought in recent years to focus its energies on its role as a place of welcome, especially for tourists. Increasingly attention has been paid to its relationship to the castle keep and to the possibility of establishing a coherent medieval district within the city centre. It is also charged with being the focus of the bishop's teaching ministry in the diocese. This has led it to see how best it can use its building as a catalyst for education and learning.

No church has a monopoly on any of these issues; each shares with its neighbours, with ecumenical partners and with others of goodwill in a common responsibility for the wellbeing of the city and for all who make up its common life.

These priorities are worked out in practice in a number of different ways.

Ministry of welcome

Welcome is a major dimension in the life of all the city centre churches. Each church is kept open throughout the week, offering a place of peace and an opportunity for reflection. This is a particular feature of the ministry at St John. At the cathedral informal opportunities are made for visitors to leave prayers and light candles, as well as some provision for a personal welcome. For example, there is always a verger on duty and, especially in summer months, volunteer 'welcomers' are on hand to answer questions and point people in the right direction.

While there can be no doubt that regular congregations have declined, there is strong evidence of the popularity of churches as places to visit and tourism has come to be seen as an increasingly important dimension to the church's ministry over the past decade or more. It is estimated that some 50,000 people pass through the doors of the cathedral alone each year.

It is important to respond creatively to the opportunities that this affords. Interpretation is an important issue. In a largely secular and multi-cultural society it can no longer be taken for granted that visitors to churches will be able to 'read' the building or understand the symbolic language evident in monuments and artefacts and in its very structure and layout. If tourists are to gain something from their visit they need interpretative tools. There is much talk about turning 'tourists into pilgrims', but only when the gap in understanding is fully appreciated can the task of informal education be undertaken adequately.

Part of the response to visitors is the provision of appropriate facilities. There is an expectation that 'attractions' will offer something to eat and drink, an opportunity to purchase gifts or souvenirs, a toilet. It is not viable or feasible for every church to meet these needs but the cathedral does, and part of its plans for the future includes investment in these areas.

It no longer makes sense for churches to operate independently. Collaboration and partnership are the order of the day with other churches and with secular agencies. St Andrew (whose Parish Priest is also City Centre Chaplain) acts as a base for the chaplaincy, offering office and meeting space in its hall. St Thomas, having hosted the Children's Society for a number of years, now has plans to offer accommodation to a number of agencies as part of its planned redevelopment, providing both income and also fulfilling its wider mission. St John's hall is used regularly by a number of groups, including the Harbour Project for Asylum Seekers and the Compassionate Friends for bereaved parents.

Meanwhile the cathedral is heading a partnership ('The Heart of the City') with the City Council and the Society of Antiquaries (who administer the castle keep) which seeks to renew the historic medieval core of the city to bring a renewed focus and sense of identity to one of its most important areas.

Culture and community

Despite the failure of the Newcastle-Gateshead bid to become European City of Culture, 'culture' in its broadest sense has remained on the city's agenda as a key driver of urban renewal. The unique ambience and acoustics offered by the historic centre churches have made them obvious venues for choral music, organ recitals and other performing arts. St John and the cathedral have their own strong choral traditions. The cathedral choir has performed with the Northern Sinfonia at The Sage Gateshead and in the cathedral itself. The importance of reciprocity and an attention to the setting clearly play their part in this process (there is also no organ at The Sage). More work needs to be done to foster existing relationships and to create new partnerships.

The churches themselves are living galleries of craftsmanship and creativity, indeed they might be seen as works of art in their own right. They also offer space for temporary exhibitions and installations. The celebration of human creativity may be seen as a celebration of God's gifts to creation.

Culture is broader than the celebration of music or of visual art. Critics of Newcastle-Gateshead's failed Capital of Culture bid pointed to a narrow understanding of culture as high art at the expense of a recognition of more popular expressions of human exchange.

This objection may also be levelled at the churches. The Church of England is sometimes prone to cultural elitism, and in a city where over 50,000 people regularly pass through the gates of St James's Park to support Newcastle United ('The Toon'), it remains a challenge to connect with the aspirations of more than a small minority.

Likewise, how are the churches to respond to one of the key cultural dynamics of Newcastle's emerging economic life – as a 'party city'? The city centre comes alive at night when the churches are, for the most part, closed. Is there a role for the Church which takes seriously this phenomenon without necessarily colluding with every aspect of it? The cathedral is situated at the south end of the Bigg Market and copes with the 'morning after' fallout and detritus. Could it respond more proactively and, if so, how? In several Scandinavian cities, cathedrals and city centre churches have developed the concept of 'night church', in which buildings stay open as havens of peace and reflection, for simple worship and for counselling. Could this model be applied to Newcastle?

Learning

The churches of Newcastle bear silent testimony in stone, glass and wood, through their ornaments, works of art and monuments, not only to the faith of the Church but also to the story of the city. Guides and various forms of signage and interpretation help to articulate that story and make connections with the faith community. Additionally, the opportunity to leave prayers and light candles offers a sense of the spiritual purpose to which these buildings testify. These may engage visitors in a kind of 'informal' learning. But this is only a part of the story. In its own way, each of the city churches has developed an educational role appropriate to its own context, its priorities and the opportunities presented to it. St Ann to the east of the city centre holds an annual lecture involving a high-profile speaker. The City Centre Chaplaincy at St Andrew offers a number of breakfast 'conversations' and lunchtime talks. These are designed both to fit the rhythms of city centre life and also to focus on subjects that are of relevance to the business and commercial community. St Thomas has built on its links with the staff-student communities at the two universities, its connections with the Civic Centre and its radical traditions to focus (through lectures and worship-based events) on issues such as justice and fair trade. Its One World Shop is in itself an obvious example of informal education. Its regular 'Breathing Space' attracts people to worship and reflection beyond the forms of conventional Anglican liturgy.

School visits are a regular dimension of the cathedral's educational work. Many of these are self-guided and some involve volunteers from the cathedral community but a highpoint is the annual 'At Home with St Nicholas' – a week in which some 700 children from schools across the region engage in a series of activities, including a 'living history trail', in which characters from Newcastle's past share their part in the city's story, and craft activities related to the themes of the visit.

The cathedral has ambitious plans to develop this work, inspired by its dedication to St Nicholas, Patron Saint of Children, to focus on the theology and spirituality of childhood. The St Nicholas Centre is intended to provide a place of research and reflection as well as to offer examples of good practice, for example in the provision of a dedicated 'Godly Play' classroom. An exhibition of the iconography of St Nicholas, which traced the development of the fourth-century saint into Santa Claus, and a series of conversations on the future of childhood marked a beginning of this exploration. While many of these developments are still in the planning stage, funds have already been raised to refurbish and re-equip the former choir vestry as a multi-purpose educational facility.

Conclusion

Buildings in themselves may be splendid, interesting, quaint or disturbing, but it is the living community that gives them meaning and purpose.

The churches of Newcastle are part of the city's architectural richness and heritage. However, it is in their work and through the faith communities that inhabit them that they make their most significant contribution to the life of the city. The challenge for the churches is both to take seriously their stewardship of these remarkable buildings and also to reflect imaginatively on the context in which they are set and the wider communities they serve, in order to offer a renewed sense of mission for buildings that were created in a different age and within a different culture.

At best, the city's churches are iconic structures which may act as a springboard for mission. Like the faith to which they witness their roots are in the past, but over centuries of use they have proven adaptable to new circumstances. In some ways they challenge prevailing utilitarian assumptions; they furnish glimpses of gratuitous beauty and can seem sublimely impractical. They have also continued to offer space for people to meet, to celebrate, to explore and to reflect. They are venues, destinations, and players in the commercial, cultural and educational life of the city. They inhabit the borderlands between the sacred and secular. They are holy yet human institutions which continue to capture the imagination and challenge the presumptions of those who encounter them. They continue to evolve and develop, to find new opportunities for witness and service. Even in a city where new landscapes are being created and new structures added year by year, it is the enduring importance of the churches of Newcastle that offers both structure and continuity to the fabric of the place.

FIVE

A SENSE OF PLACE: FOUR TOURIST TRAILS

CYRIL WINSKELL

Here are four 'tourist trails'. Two are short urban walks and two are tours by car through the ever-changing Northumbrian countryside.

The descriptions are deliberately and unashamedly personal. They are primarily Cyril Winskell's in conversation, on site, with Helen Savage. Our hope and expectation are that you will agree with some of our observations and will strongly react against others, but, more importantly, that you will not only enjoy exploring a dozen or so fine and very different churches but will also think about the role each plays in the town and landscape in which it is set. Churches are not built in isolation from the communities which they serve; they also reflect those communities, their values and priorities. Their history is an inextricable part of the communities of which they are part.

The trails are not intended to be comprehensive. We hope that you will adapt them and add to them as you wish, and that you will refer to the gazetteer at the back of this book for fuller and rather more objective information about each church.

Our choice of destinations may seem a little perverse. Why, for example, have we not included the obvious sites of Holy Island and Bamburgh? The answer, simply, is that information about these is already easy to find. We very much hope you'll want to explore many more churches than those we include in these trails. We hope that you'll visit Warkworth and stroll through Alnwick, that you'll want to go and see the high Victorian and sharply contrasting splendour of the two great St George's: Cullercoats and Newcastle (Jesmond); we hope that you'll enjoy discovering the quiet rural charm of the churches of the Wansbeck Valley in mid-Northumberland. In fact we hope that you'll use the gazetteer to map out very many voyages of discovery.

Our great delight was to visit places we thought we knew well and find that, as we looked and talked, we saw them in a new light – and with that, we enjoyed much food for thought.

TRAIL 1: NEWCASTLE: ST ANDREW (NEWGATE STREET) TO ST NICHOLAS CATHEDRAL

A very leisurely stroll through the city of Newcastle, which should take little more than an hour.

Begin the walk at the gate into St Andrew's churchyard on the south side of Gallowgate, where the medieval town wall has been breached. Look to your left and notice the astonishing and quite bizarre Victorian overbuilding of the wall. The opposite stretch of wall, running south-westwards and parallel to Stowell Street is, in contrast, well preserved.

THE CRYPT.   ST NICHOLAS CATHEDRAL

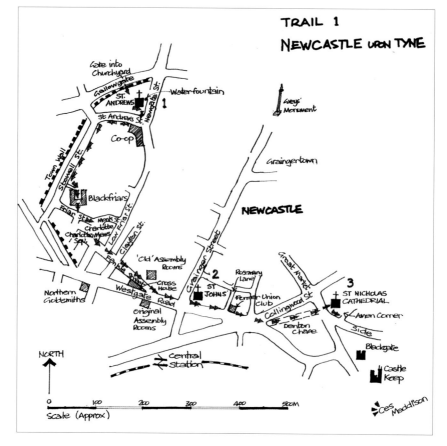

The churchyard has some fine grave monuments and includes near the south porch that of the celebrated Newcastle composer and organist Charles Avison (1709-70). Notice the unusual stone roof of the chancel porch (also on the south side of the building).

Turn left into Newgate Street and view a fine restored Victorian water-fountain in the east boundary wall of St Andrew's. Before turning about into Darn Crook, now St Andrew's Street, spare a few moments to look at the splendid late art deco Co-op building. It retains many splendid details, including the iron handrails to the stone staircases.

Turn left into Stowell Street. This area, at the junction of Stowell Street and Darn Crook, was once a place of markets, where fish and fresh produce were auctioned in the still unusually grand pubs. Stowell Street grew as a centre of trade and manufacturing; it has now become Newcastle's Chinatown (notice the flamboyant Chinese gate). The town walls can be glimpsed again at the south end of the street, but well before then turn left through an opening in the street onto the site of Blackfriars.

Only the foundations of the thirteenth-century Dominican friary church can be traced, but the rather special monastic buildings on its south side remain, which after the Dissolution were leased to nine of the town's craft companies. They now house a restaurant, a number of craft workshops and the North of England Civic Trust.

Leave the site through the passage in the south-east side of the cloister into Monk Street and cross Charlotte Mews into Charlotte Square, laid out by William Newton (architect of the Assembly Rooms, where he lived). Turn left in Fenkle Street. On the left notice Low Friar Street which is composed of eighteenth-century buildings which no longer have a back lane! Clayton Street, which represents the last part of Richard Grainger's great development in Newcastle, and which was finished in about 1839 shortly before he was declared bankrupt, is built right against the backs of the buildings along the earlier street. The Victorian developers had little respect for the medieval street plan of the city.

As you cross Clayton Street along Fenkle Street, you can glimpse the spire of St Mary's Cathedral to your right, and also the Golden Lady and its fine matching clock sculpted by Glover onto the Northern Goldsmiths building on the corner of Westgate Road, designed by R. Burns Dick in the 1920s.

The imposing 'Old' Assembly Rooms on the north side of Fenkle Street were built in 1776 to replace older assembly rooms, a fine stone building which stands on the south side of Westgate Road – almost opposite. The 1776 hall was designed as a grand venue at which Northumberland gentlemen could bring their daughters out into society (and where Cyril met his wife in 1959).

Continue eastwards into Westgate Road and to St John's Church on the corner of Grainger Street. From here look up the street to Grainger's monument to Lord Grey and, in the opposite direction, right to Central Station, planned but not completed by John Dobson. The portico was completed faithfully by Prosser in 1863 to Dobson's design. Look back, westwards along Westgate Road, and notice one of the most amazing corners in Newcastle – dominated by Cross House, built in Portland limestone, quite foreign to the town but fine nonetheless.

After pausing to look around St John's, continue eastwards along Westgate Road and notice the recent decorative inscriptions in the kerbstones. Across the street to the south is the superb medley of the Mining Institute and the earlier Literary and Philosophical Society built in 1822-5. The architect was John Green. On the north of the street, immediately to the east of St John's, on the corner of Rosemary Lane, is the exuberant French-style neo-baroque former Union Club, now a pub.

Cross Westgate Road and ignore Collingwood Street, a rather clumsy nineteenth-century by-pass, and approach St Nicholas Cathedral along Denton Chare, a narrow (only about 3m wide) but (sometimes) remarkably sunny passage. This leads right to the west door of the cathedral. Before entering the cathedral, look right to the Keep and the Black Gate of the Norman castle. Before the High Level Bridge was built, the old Great North Road ran up the hill of the Side, past the west door of the cathedral and into the Groat, Cloth and Bigg Markets, where fine old coaching-houses still survive – though put to a very different use.

There is much to admire in the cathedral, but the simple, unadorned fourteenth-century crypt is special. It is a place of absolute tranquillity and a focus of spirituality in the very heart of the city that never ceases to amaze.

On the south side of the cathedral notice how the eighteenth-century building has been tacked onto it. Such development could never now be contemplated and yet, in a strange way, it does not seem out of place. It rather illustrates the nature of change and diversity which come together through no grand plan but typify a city that grows and is alive and even mirrors our very selves. We sometimes need to accept confusion. It is part of us.

TRAIL 2: THE TYNE VALLEY

A trail by car and on foot: a little over 2 hours.

This trail could start further east along the Tyne at Ovingham, but this might be to over-egg the cake: the three sites of Bywell, Corbridge and Hexham together provide a richly satisfying whole.

Bywell has two churches – both are exceptional, but only one, St Peter, is used regularly for worship. Begin here. (To find Bywell turn off the A69 (southwards) onto the B6309; follow the signs towards Stocksfield and in the valley bottom, just past the junction with the road from Ovington, turn right to Bywell – a no-through road.) Park at the end of the road outside the gate to St Peter. There is so much to admire here, but notice the way in which the three long lancet windows in the east end of the choir have been built almost by rule of thumb and are slightly irregular. This in no way detracts from their splendour.

The lovely churchyard is informal and seems to have been almost landscaped into the hill. This informality is in contrast to the rather formal approach to the west of the church with its drive and neatly manicured hedges, all set within parkland. The overall effect, in summer or winter, is peaceful and green.

Leave the car and walk back to the stone cross on the drive and left to St Andrew. This precious building, with its superb Saxon tower, represents a model for the maintenance of a redundant but highly significant church. Not only is the building beautiful but it has been restored in an exemplary manner.

The interior is much more intimate than that of St Peter – it almost has the feel of a private chapel and yet is so complete. Notice the unusually small pews which use so much of the available space!

As you leave Bywell, don't follow the road sign (on your left) to Corbridge, but turn right over Bywell Bridge, past Stocksfield Station, and take the A695 through Riding Mill towards Hexham. Fork right into Corbridge, cross the Tyne and take the second left into Middle Street. St Andrew's Church is in the Market Square.

NORTH TRANSEPT AND
NORTH AISLE, CHANCEL, HEXHAM ABBEY

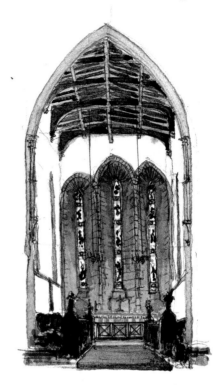

ST PETERS BYWELL

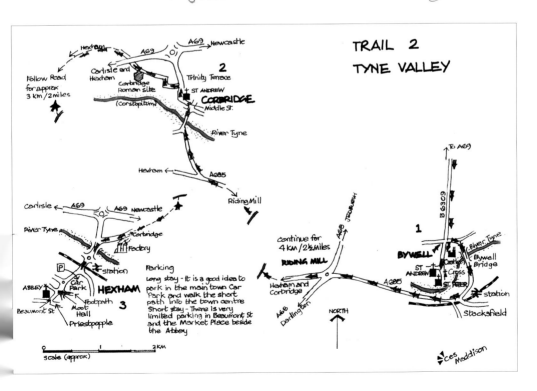

TRAIL 2
TYNE VALLEY

Parking
Long stay - It is a good idea to park in the main town Car Park and walk the short path into the town centre
Short stay - There is very limited parking in Beaumont St and the Market Place beside the Abbey

scale (approx)

Corbridge epitomises a sense of urban space. The built form is all on a human scale and reflects centuries of use. The diversity and confusion of the town strongly contrasts with the rural parkland of Bywell. There is a cacophony of street signage – omnipresent but regrettable, and, perhaps, an inevitable by-product of a democratic society in which people expect and demand information.

In the heart of the town, as in Newcastle, the church is now separated from the market-place by a busy road. As you step through the lych-gate the effect is Tardis-like, of entering another and far more tranquil world. It is an amazing contrast.

Inside St Andrew there are again so many things to admire. Notice the rare consistency of the columns in the nave. Despite its palimpsest of building styles it is an easy building to 'read' and to understand. Everything is in place and the use of the building for liturgy is made plain.

The millennium window in the spacious north transept makes striking use of uncoloured glass and it is a joy (and unusual) to see plain glass too in the south wall of the chancel. It gives a welcome clarity.

The pele tower in the churchyard is very fine, but notice how the church was approached from a number of points – each entrance tells the story of the significance of its place in the town. As you walk around the roads outside the churchyard, notice the early fourteenth-century King's Oven set into the wall opposite the west end of the church – a priceless treasure to find in a street!

Take the road north out of the Market Square and then turn left (towards Beaufront) along Trinity Terrace. This back road into Hexham takes you past the Roman site of *Corstopitum*, just to the east of modern Corbridge. This imposing and surprisingly cosmopolitan Roman town is far more significant than just as a quarry from which to build Corbridge Church and Hexham Abbey, and merits a leisurely visit. Remains of only part of the town centre can now be seen, but these are more than sufficient to give an impression of its size and status.

In Hexham, find your way up to the abbey, which again is built beside a market-place – a lovely setting at the heart of a much bigger, more bustling town than Corbridge. Hexham has a county town feel – even though it is not such.

The abbey was much restored in the nineteenth century. The west end by John Dobson, facing the market-place, adds little to the distinction of the building.

As you enter the doorway into the 'slype' (the east side of the south porch) notice how the window above it looks directly to the town gate in the medieval Moot Hall across the market-place – a careful watch can be kept!

In the porch the modern blue glass includes very sensitively-done calligraphy. This is part of a very good modern intervention in which the recent work appears to be almost detached from the ancient stonework.

Inside the building, the attention is first captured by the wonderful 'Night Stair' leading down into the south transept. The Early English transepts themselves, like the lancet windows at Bywell, betray an engaging number of minor irregularities. This evidence of a 'rule of thumb' approach to building is comforting. Like the modern townscape, it reflects the imperfection of our lives. In contrast, the heavy-handed Victorian nave by Temple Moore seems far too regular and impersonal.

Hexham Abbey is a treasure-house and well repays time spent wandering through it slowly. Not all its gems are ancient (though the crypt is very special); good modern details include the millennium tapestry on the south wall of the nave, the portable nave altar and the peaceful chapel for private prayer in the north-east corner. The high altar has a unique dignity in the diocese in its size and scale and the splendid organ again exemplifies the way in which modern work can be placed on and within an ancient setting.

TRAIL 3: MORPETH

A leisurely walk through a market town (roughly 45 minutes)

The walk begins at the ancient parish church of the town, St Mary's, which can be found south of the town centre on the west side of the old Great North Road (A197). The lych-gate marks a pleasant, almost rural, approach to the church. A feeling of rural tranquillity is even more apparent as you walk around the south side of the building. Even when the building is locked (it usually is) it is possible to appreciate the consistent Early English style of its architecture, rare in the diocese. It makes a pleasing whole. Notice too how the building, both nave and chancel, has been re-roofed – and lowered. The marks of older roofs can be clearly seen by the water tabling on the exposed gables.

Leave the church by the lych-gate again and turn left. Take the path that rises to the left above the road (just past the Sun Inn) and walk into the town parallel to the Great North Road but above it. The path rejoins the road just above Morpeth Court House, built by John Dobson in the 1820s. It is the control-house of the gaol which once lay behind it – a huge concentric plan of buildings. Dobson loved castellation and used it here rather heavy-handedly.

ST JAMES, MORPETH LOOKING TO COLONNADE.

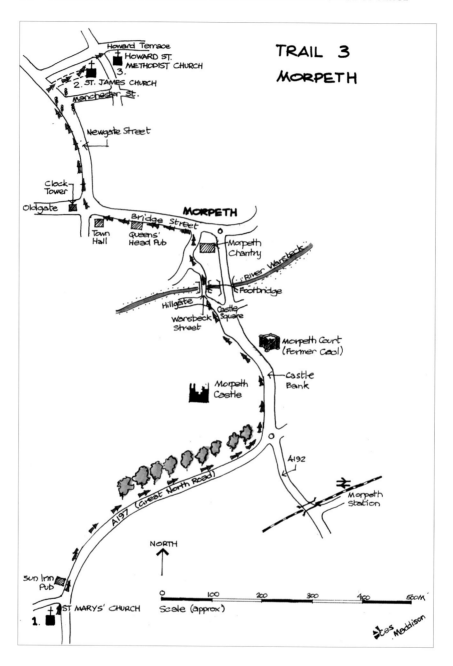

Turn left into Castle Square and then right into Wansbeck Street. The buildings here have a thoroughly domestic feel and reflect details on a human scale such as the width of the paths and gates. Cross the River Wansbeck by the charming 1869 footbridge and glimpse finer buildings on the streets beyond.

Immediately beyond the bridge, pass Morpeth Chantry (formerly All Saints Church). It is good to see the building still in use and open. Note the plaque on the west end commemorating the 'father of English botany', William Turner (1508-68), who was educated here.

As you come into Bridge Street, turn left. So many of the shop fronts here are recent. Within 10 years it will undoubtedly look quite different but the basic form of the street will remain. Notice the fine Queen's Head Hotel and then especially the Town Hall, the most important building in the street, designed by Vanbrugh in 1714. It was severely damaged by fire and largely rebuilt in 1869-70 by R.J. Johnson but contains a fine staircase.

The Clock Tower at the head of Oldgate is a landmark and still determines the transport routes in its own time. It seems to have a defensive quality.

Carry on right into Newgate Street. There is a lovely variety of buildings here. The front-ages are built on multiples of a standard size and most buildings carry three storeys, but there is a range of different roof heights. Little ginnels give access to backyards. In the twentieth century in many other towns these were filled in. A great mistake – they add texture and interest to a street.

Just beyond the traffic-lights and the junction with Manchester Street, approach the church of St James through the colonnade on the street front. This is a façade which again provides an entry to a different and more tranquil world. The church itself lies at the end of an impressive avenue of trees. St James, like St Mary, impresses with its sense of completeness, but it is much later – built in the 1840s by Ferrey, who also designed the fittings inside the building. Few modern architects are allowed to exercise such a comprehensive design on a church. Ferrey's work is less severe and far more pleasing than Temple Moore's efforts at Hexham Abbey.

End the walk by noting Howard Street Methodist Church, just beyond St James. This is a classic design of a hall of teaching rooms and was completed in 1905. A few details of original glass remain. It is a great pity that in the recent necessary remodelling of the building steps that once led up to the main door have been removed – they added scale and dignity to the building.

TRAIL 4: THE BORDERS

A trail by car, lasting roughly two hours.

The broad skies above the Tweed Valley have a uniquely luminous quality, even when it is cloudy, as it often is. The trail begins in the heart of the valley at the parish church of Norham, St Cuthbert, which is set at the west end of the village (at the opposite end from the castle) within a huge churchyard. One is struck immediately by the extraordinary length of the building – and by the large, rather incongruous, double bellcote.

Inside, the majesty of the great round columns of the southern arcade are most impressive, though the nineteenth-century octagonal columns of the north arcade are less so. The lack of a chancel step only adds to the impression of length (curiously, the building seems longer when one looks from east to west than from west to east).

These days, the quality of the stonework in a building like St Cuthbert is often a matter for comment, but what would the original twelfth-century church have been like when it was painted in its original, presumably gaudy, colours?!

The purity of design diminishes as you move east in the chancel. The sanctuary is a disappointment. The sanctuary steps seem presumptive and the east end is just stuck on.

The seventeenth-century furniture, brought from Durham Cathedral, is remarkable: the pulpit, the great table at the west end of the nave and the royal armorial bearings set in the tower.

As you leave Norham, take the road south-east towards Berwick (B6470). After 1.75 miles cross the main Coldstream to Berwick Road (A698) and follow the road to Ancroft (a further 6 miles). At the east end of the village turn right onto the B6525 towards Lowick and Wooler and after 300m turn left onto the track that leads to St Anne's Church.

From outside Ancroft, St Anne is a splendid sight. Its chief glory is the remarkable tower – a pele, with beside it in the south wall of the nave a fine, early blocked doorway. Inside, the church is very plain. There are, however, rather nice encaustic tiles in the floor of the chancel. There is no sanctuary step. Much of the glass is very disappointing, plain and of poor quality. The chancel at least shows some care in the working of the corbels, each of which is different.

ST ANNE'S ANCROFT.   Gilmington 23 06 06

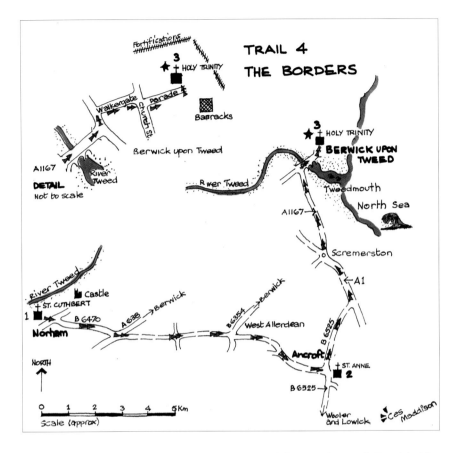

After visiting St Anne's turn right onto the B6525 and drive north towards Berwick. After a mile or two join the A1 and then at the first roundabout a mile or so further on, turn right onto the A1167 and follow the road through Tweedmouth and over the bridge into Berwick. This remarkable border town has a wonderful mix of buildings. The pantiles (once used for ballast) and painted walls typical of the North-East coast abound, but Berwick does not feel at all English.

Holy Trinity, the parish church, is set in the north-east part of the old town, just inside the walls (from the bridge turn left into Marygate, right into Walkergate, right into Church Street and then left onto the Parade). It is a marvellous building. The fineness of the walls is astonishing and the crispness of the mouldings is evidence of truly serious endeavour. It seems strange to find such a building in Northumberland – it has a real urban quality that contrasts strongly with the many beautiful rural churches of the diocese, which seem rustic in comparison. The only really jarring note is the reredos (itself a fine work by the young Lutyens), which makes nonsense of the east window.

The finesse of the building is apparent outside too, with a delicate negative moulding that gives a sophisticated texture to the stonework. The churchyard is remarkably well-ordered with an unusual number of table graves.

Beyond Holy Trinity, the other buildings in the spacious townscape are a pleasing mixture of dignity and graciousness. The neighbouring churches are all also very fine, each in its own style.

SIX

STAINED GLASS AND
OTHER FURNISHINGS

NEIL MOAT

The churches of the Anglican Diocese of Newcastle offer the stained-glass enthusiast a feast. Much of this glass is from the nineteenth and twentieth centuries and is of a remarkably high standard. Several complete schemes of glazing and many individual windows are outstanding.

Too often these windows are little understood, and their potential as mediators of religious experience and truth under-appreciated. The impact of windows should not be under-estimated. It is indeed remarkable how even a single one – such as Wilhelmina Geddes's monumental *Crucifixion* at Wallsend, St Luke – can reduce a large and noisy party of visitors to stupefied silence and awe.

There was certainly stained glass in our churches during the high medieval period, but precious little of it has survived.[1] Northumberland has the greater share of what does survive in the North-East. Much of this amounts to tantalising fragments (e.g. at Ponteland, St Mary and Bothal, St Andrew), although the diocese boasts the only substantially complete medieval window north of the Tees (albeit restored in the mid-nineteenth century), the remarkable mid-fourteenth century, five-light *Jesse Tree* at Morpeth, St Mary. Of later centuries, there is even less: only some late eighteenth-century fragments in a tiny window at Alnwick, St Michael, which may relate to the filigree 'Gothick' renovation of the church undertaken by the Adam brothers, contemporaneous with their renovations, *c.*1774, at Alnwick Castle for the chapel there. The noted Dublin-born London glass-painter James Pearson (died 1838) supplied delicate ornamental and heraldic glazing.[2]

Until the early years of the nineteenth century, stained glass in Britain remained an expensive art form, available only to the wealthy. Nevertheless, there had been a modest revival of inter-est in the medium during the eighteenth century, both for domestic and for religious settings, and despite the penalties placed on the glass trade by excise duty, which was not repealed until 1845.[3] An increase in general prosperity, the rise of the Romantic Movement and religious revivals in the Anglican and Roman Catholic churches also encouraged a marked increase in demand for new stained glass, often in a revival of medieval styles. One consequence of these developments was that stained glass was transformed from a dilettante art form into a major national industry, offering a readily affordable commodity to the burgeoning middle classes of a newly industrialised Britain – a process in which Newcastle played a ignificant role. However, it would be fair to say that the apparent artlessness of much early nineteenth-century stained glass – as an attempt to recreate the supposed 'naivety' of medieval design – is difficult for us to appreciate today (and has militated against its preservation), and these windows are perhaps chiefly of interest less in terms of art than as examples of important technical developments, and as monuments of a particular period in the history of taste.[4]

Nevertheless, some artists were capable of considerable erudition, as in the London-based Thomas Willement's remarkable east windows for Cresswell, St Bartholomew (1836-9): the figure scenes here ape Anglo-Saxon, Anglo-Norman and high medieval manuscript illumination, although the white, gold and sky-blue colour scheme is more closely reminiscent of Romanesque enamelled metalwork than of stained glass. A number of windows by the Newcastle-based William Wailes are also notable, for example his apse windows (1844-6) for the neo-Norman church of Morpeth, St James or the ritual east window (also 1844) at Sugley, Holy Saviour. The Sugley window seamlessly combines a fourteenth-century manner (derived from the nave windows at York Minster) with a sweetly Italianate ('Botticellian') figure style. His 1842 south-west transept window at Newcastle, St Nicholas (now Newcastle Cathedral) is an equally remarkable evocation of English fifteenth-century glazing.

William Wailes (1808-81) is the paradigm of the successful nineteenth-century stained-glass manufacturer. He entered the stained-glass market in 1836. By 1841 he had opened his new stained-glass works in Bath Lane, Newcastle, where they were to remain until their demise during the First World War. The terminology is in itself significant, signifying a factory, not an artist's studio – and few churches in the kingdom were to escape hosting a Wailes window!

His early collaboration with the important Gothic Revival architect A.W.N. Pugin (between late 1841 and late 1845) made Wailes's reputation, and he became a glazier of choice for such major figures in the architectural world as William Butterfield, George Gilbert Scott and George Edmund Street. But Wailes was not the first to 'revive' the 'lost art' of stained glass in Newcastle; that accolade should perhaps be given to John Gibson (1794-1854). As early as 1827 Gibson had provided a new east window for Newcastle, St Nicholas (now lost). Parts of an exactly contemporary version of the same design survive at Stockton-on-Tees, St Thomas. Time has not been kind to Gibson's glass. His windows for Greenhead (1827) and Walker (1849) parish churches have been lost, and those for Elsdon, St Cuthbert (c.1837), and two Newcastle churches – St John (c.1827) and St Andrew (1844) – survive only in fragments.

None of these works were as successfully medieval in spirit as Wailes's stained glass, although his set (1851 onwards) for the chancel of Bamburgh, St Aidan is recorded as having been modelled after the sixteenth-century glass of St Jacques, Liège (Belgium).[5]

Although Victorian stained glass is often thought of as offering only a pale imitation of the 'glories' of the Middle Ages, the best of the nineteenth-century commercial studios adopted a creative engagement with the past, extending and developing a wide range of English and Continental exemplars. Particularly good are Clayton and Bell's east windows (1860) at St Lawrence, Warkworth, and C.E. Kempe and Co.'s complete chancel set (1883-4) at Embleton, Holy Trinity.[6] Both firms were major (and influential) London studios, much favoured in the diocese. Local, mostly Newcastle-based firms such as Henry Mark Barnett, George Joseph Baguley (and Sons) and Atkinson Bros (and into the twentieth century, Elders Walker and Reed, Millican and Co.) also did a great deal of creditable work in the region.

Unease in the British arts establishment with the incessant commercialisation of the decorative arts increasingly led to calls for reform, culminating in the English 'Arts and Crafts' movement. One welcome result was the reaffirmation of the status of stained glass as a high-class art form in its own right – and the ideal of the individual artist-craftsman (or woman) is still very much the reality for many practising stained-glass artists to this day.

The diocese possesses several excellent examples of this developing process: Morris and Co.'s (i.e. William Morris, Edward Burne-Jones and Ford Madox Brown) Italianate east window (1872) for Haltwhistle, Holy Cross;[7] Daniel Cottier and Co.'s Japanese inflected north aisle window (1871) for Cramlington, St Nicholas; Henry Ellis Wooldridge's delicately coloured neo-Grecian designs for Alston, St Augustine (1872) and Alnwick, St Michael (1871), and Charles Hardgrave's beautiful *Resurrection* (1883) for Bywell, St Andrew.[8]

Especially worthy examples of Arts and Crafts-style glass proper include Henry Payne's *Noah* (1908) at Tynemouth, Holy Saviour; James Eadie-Reid's *Dorcas and Her Disciples* (1903) for Corbridge, St Andrew and Caroline Townshend's windows for Newcastle Cathedral (1907), and Morpeth, St Mary (1929). In Newcastle, St George (1887-90) and Fenham, St James and St Basil (1928-32) the diocese possesses two outstanding buildings, both sumptuously furnished and glazed as complete artistic entities and representative respectively of the Arts and Crafts movement in its early, experimental and later 'establishment' phases.[9]

The Arts and Crafts movement shaded over into the first stirrings of modernism with the remarkable windows, commissioned from the Dublin-based crafts-workers' guild *An Túr Gloine* ('The Tower of Glass'),[10] for the two main parish churches of Wallsend – the only representative collection of modern Irish stained glass on the mainland of Britain. Michael Healey's set at St Peter's will readily elicit the response 'bejewelled',[11] but it is Wilhelmina Geddes's emotionally raw, and profoundly moving, *Crucifixion* (1921-2) at St Luke's, (commissioned as the parish war memorial), that will haunt the visitor's memory.[12] Indeed, the requirement for appropriate memorials to the dead of the First World War called forth some quite remarkable commissions: Martin Travers's east windows for North Shields, St Augustin, installed between 1922 and 1927, are an especially notable early example of the work of this important designer. Richard George Hatton's glittering *Crucifixion* for Shilbottle, St James (1919-21) is also worthy of note.[13] Equally fine, although more traditional in style, are James Eadie-Reid's east window at Ashington, Holy Sepulchre (1923) and the complete scheme of glazing for Jesmond, Holy Trinity (1920-2) by the A.K. Nicholson Studios (London).

Modernism as such made fewer converts – although Frank Barber's four little panels (1931) in the crypt of Newcastle Cathedral are remarkable enough, primitive and decorative in the manner of Matisse or Chagall.[14]

The diocese did not escape the failure of nerve and of emotional commitment that has beset so much British stained glass since the Second World War. Harry Stammer's jolly east window (1961) for Wooler, St Mary, and Lawrence Lee's kaleidoscopic east window for Jesmond Parish Church (1956) are perhaps the best of a rather lacklustre bunch.

The region is fortunate to have possessed two stained-glass artists whose works ran somewhat counter to the national trend: Stanley Murray Scott (1912-97) and Leonard Charles Evetts (1909-97).

Scott was born in Sunderland and received his artistic training at Sunderland and Newcastle. For almost the entirety of his career (from 1933) he was principal artist at Reed Millican and Co., for whom he designed and executed a great deal of creditable work throughout the north. Primarily a figurative artist, Scott possessed a fine sense of colour and design. Good early examples of his work can be seen at North Shields, St Augustin (1936 and 1938), whilst the pair of windows at Shotley, St John (1956 and 1958) are particularly subtle in their use of materials. Late in his career he essayed a number of excellent abstract designs notable for their adoption of a fully Modernist idiom, as in the pair for the nave aisle of Hexham Abbey (1965 and 1972) and an excellent two-light design (1971) in the north transept of the cathedral.

The stained-glass work of Evetts has tended, perhaps unfairly, to overshadow that of Scott. Evetts was born in Newport (Wales) and trained at the Royal College of Art (London). From 1937 until 1974 he was lecturer in design at the King Edward VII School of Art, King's College, Newcastle (now the School of Fine Arts at the University of Newcastle upon Tyne), although he continued to work in stained glass until the very end. He was always a versatile artist and his ruggedly robust stained glass – seemingly so at one with the Northumbrian landscape and character – conceals a deep respect for historical tradition, as in his development of the supposedly vernacular 'Northumbrian' plain-glazing style, and in his favourite red/blue-on-white colour schemes, derived from the palette of much late-medieval English stained glass. Of the many windows commissioned from the late-1940s onwards, the two in the cathedral (1958 and 1962) must stand as representative examples of Evetts's wide range. One is an inventive exercise in plain-glazing, the other works on several different scales and makes effective use of the long view down the cathedral aisle.

Only time will tell whether the successors to Scott and Evetts can create works of art able to endure in our affections. There have been some interesting developments of late, but it would be invidious, at this moment, to single out any one artist for particular comment. However, if there is one plea that I would make, it is for the recapture of that sense of stained glass as a high-status art form and not as the ecclesiastical equivalent of second-rate poster art. True, the pictorial aspect is an important component, but stained glass is even more a creative exercise in the manipulation of light and colour, glass and metalwork and the visual textures of surfaces within an architectural (and liturgical) setting. Why else commission a window? As Christopher Whall (the father of the modern British school of stained-glass design) once remarked, 'Keep your pictures for the walls and your windows for the holes in them'.[15]

Whall's dictum invites reflection on the right means to decorate and enhance the architectural setting of our worship. Only the merest scraps of painted wall decorations survive from before the nineteenth century amongst the diocese's churches.

The more elaborate 'ecclesiological' interiors of the early nineteenth century were intended to revive the presumed appearance of lost medieval glories, with new stained glass, murals, stencilling and tiling frequently considered together as elements in one decorative (often brightly coloured) continuum. Although several such schemes are known to have existed in the diocese, none now survive save for their tiled floors. Of particular note in this respect are the sanctuary pavements at Stamfordham, St Mary (1848 with rare tiles by Chamberlain's of Worcester),[16] Meldon, St John (1849 with tiles by Minton and Co. after designs by A.W.N. Pugin) and Morpeth, St James (1844-6, donated by Herbert Minton himself), an especially extensive and elaborate example.

Later church interiors in the diocese, whether Anglo-Catholic or evangelical, have tended towards a studied refinement and restraint, often based on late-medieval English exemplars (although far less colourful), with much use of plain and carved oak for panelling, furniture and roofs, whitewashed walls, and simple tiled floors (with now and then an outbreak of marble or mosaic) – a taste which persisted well into the twentieth century. Clayton and Bell's 'spirit' frescoes around the apse of Morpeth, St James (1875), and Kempe and Co.'s stencilled decorations at Haltwhistle, Holy Cross (1881), are therefore somewhat outside the regional norm. Both schemes survive only in part, and have been the subject of recent conservation projects. The chancel roof at Haltwhistle is a particularly effective evocation of the decorated timberwork of our late-medieval churches. It was not unusual for many of the larger commercial stained-glass firms of the nineteenth century to offer a fully comprehensive church decorating service. Kempe and Co. also supplied statuary, as in their painted alabaster reredos at Haltwhistle.

Early in the twentieth century, the Parisian-trained artist James Eadie-Reid worked with the Newcastle-based woodcarving workshop of Ralph Hedley, and together they created a number of impressive ensembles for northern churches. These combined painted panels and deeply carved reliefs for altars and reredoses with extensive mural schemes, of which that at Newcastle, St Gabriel (1906) is an excellent example. In a particularly interesting development, the Newcastle-based architectural practice of Hicks and Charlewood pursued a revival of Anglo-Saxon ornament (thus invoking the heroic age of Northumbrian Christianity), as in their remarkable stencilled ceilings for Benwell, St James (1901-2) and the Bishop's Throne – in oak inlaid with coloured gesso relief – for Morpeth, St James (1925).

There remains one remarkable interior amongst the diocese's churches which is singularly worthy of note – that at Newcastle, St George (Jesmond) one of the great 'might-have-beens' of ecclesiological history, whose potential influence was stalled by the increasing conservatism of Anglican taste. Here, the dazzling chancel – all marble and brass, gilt and blue mosaic, elaborately painted tiles, stained glass and stencilled ceilings, and everywhere the writhing, sinuous lines of acanthus and chrysanthemum – is perhaps the most sustainedly decorated space of all our northern churches, eruditely combining ancient symbolism and the most up-to-date of artistic styles. St George's was clearly intended, in a progressive Arts and Crafts spirit, as a manifesto on the spiritual (and future) role of all the arts. Its chancel is as much a theatre for the soul[17] as it is a liturgical or sacramental space. As such it may yet have much to teach us.

SEVEN

CHURCHYARDS

HELEN SAVAGE

Mrs C.F. Alexander is well known as the author of *All things bright and beautiful* and *Once in Royal David's City*, but one of her hymns *Within the churchyard* (along with the original last verse of *All things bright*) has long been omitted from most hymn books. It begins like this:

> Within the churchyard, side by side,
> Are many long low graves;
> And some have stones set over them,
> On some the green grass waves.
> Full many a little Christian child,
> Woman, and man, lies there;
> And we pass near them every time
> When we go in to prayer.
> They do not hear when the great bell
> Is ringing overhead;
> They cannot rise and come to church
> With us, for they are dead.[1]

This image of the churchyard portrayed by this quaint doggerel seems timelessly familiar, but an English burial ground (or for that matter an Irish one; Mrs Alexander was, after all, the wife of a future Archbishop of Armagh) two centuries earlier would have looked very different. It is highly unlikely, for example, that it would have been marked by neat rows of tombstones. These only became popular and widespread in the eighteenth century. Before then, the churchyard would have been much less encumbered by monuments to the dead and there was far less of a sense of discrete personal space occupied by each grave. It would often have served the community in other ways – as a place for public meetings or even for markets.

Many Northumbrian churchyards, especially those in the rural part of the diocese, are very ancient indeed. In the gazetteer at the end of this book there are tantalising hints that a surprisingly large number of churches though apparently medieval may in fact have had Saxon origins. The churchyards are just as ancient, and in many cases have been used for well over a thousand years. There is good evidence that land surrounding churches was first consecrated as burial ground around the eighth century.

The establishment during the nineteenth century of cemeteries on the edge of urban areas not only further emphasised the move away from seeing church burial grounds as common space but it also distanced, in a way that was novel and strange, the familiar, everyday reminder of death that churchyards had long afforded. Until the establishment of churchyards as burial grounds the dead were not interred within British settlements, but their graves were marked alongside the main roads entering and departing from every settlement established by the Romans. The new urban cemeteries of the nineteenth century hid death away. They reinforced the idea of personal ownership of grave space and hastened the process of the privatisation and sanitisation of death that gathered pace through the twentieth century.

Mrs Alexander's hymn does not just provide a snapshot of the physical appearance of the typical early Victorian graveyard. She switches from her contemplation of the familiar scene before her to explore thoughts about life and death and what they might mean for the believer:

> But we believe a day shall come
> When all the dead will rise,
> When they who sleep down in the grass,
> Will ope again their eyes.
> For Christ our Lord was buried once,
> He died and rose again,
> He conquered death, He left the grave;
> And so will Christian men.
> So when the friends we love the best
> Lie in their churchyard bed,
> We must not cry too bitterly
> Over the happy dead;
> Because, for our dear Saviour's sake,
> Our sins are all forgiv'n;
> And Christians only fall asleep
> To wake again in Heav'n.

Any British or Irish churchyard where there are monuments from the mid-nineteenth century will show that Mrs Alexander's piety represented mainstream attitudes to death and the Christian hope of resurrection. But Victorian grave monuments express subtly different views about death from those that mark today's burials, and a century earlier than Mrs Alexander still other sentiments were popular. Gravestones can provide an extraordinarily vivid source of information about people, our own forebears, and their attitudes to life and to death.

The earliest grave monuments in English churches were usually fairly simple grave-covers or coffin lids, often inscribed with a cross. Many of these survive, and, as the gazetteer shows, can be seen in a large number of Northumberland churches, albeit removed from their original sites to safe keeping in the porch or some other part of the church. Carved effigies of the deceased of increasing sophistication are also found, but these were internal church fittings and not features of the churchyard. The churchyard was used over and over again and if and when human remains were exhumed they were placed in communal charnel pits. Charnel pits were also dug inside church buildings as was discovered, for example, during an emergency archaeological excavation of part of the nave at Bedlington, St Cuthbert in 2001. If a churchyard was deemed to have too many monuments in it, incumbents were not in the least bit squeamish about clearing them so that the ground could be used again. This practice helps to give the false impression that many Northumbrian churchyards are much more recent than they really are.

When personal grave monuments became popular in the later seventeenth, but especially the eighteenth, century, something of the vivid range of symbolism that had previously adorned the rich monuments inside churches was transferred to the churchyard. Many of these are still potent and remind us of the shortness of earthly life and the grim reality of mortality: hourglasses, scythes and even the tools used by the gravedigger. Others are less familiar now, such as the handbell, common on Northumbrian stones, once rung before a funeral.[2]

Skulls often with cross-bones were another gritty and graphic symbol of death and are very common on the earliest eighteenth-century gravestones in Northumbrian churchyards, but a curious softening gradually takes place. The cross-bones become wings and then the skull, or 'death's head', regains flesh so that the grim reminder of putrefaction becomes a cherub, a heavenly being pointing the way to resurrection life. This change is found throughout Britain and even in colonial cemeteries in New England. In and around Boston it happened a generation or two later than in southern England, but Northumberland too seemed reluctant to follow fashion. Death's heads linger in some Northumbrian cemeteries late into the century and sometimes appear on the same stone alongside cherubs (Heddon-on-the-Wall, St Andrew has several excellent examples). The distinctive style of individual local masons is very evident too – and is often delightfully rustic.

James Deetz and Edwin S. Dethlefsen who first described the process of change from death's head to cherub on stones in cemeteries in eastern Massachusetts suggest that it may reflect the gradual decline of Puritanism;[3] but the next major change seems to have much more to do with fashion than with theology. Around the end of the eighteenth century, the re-awakening of interest in Classical and Near-Eastern imagery seen in architecture and furnishing styles is reflected in gravestones of stark but elegant simplicity. Urns, veils and willow branches replace the cherubs and reflect a sombre, shadowy Graeco-Roman understanding of death.

Around the same time, epitaphs also become much more expansive and instead of simple ascriptions such as 'Here lies' or 'Here lies the body of ...' longer and more elaborate inscriptions appear. Some of these are quite startling, and none more than the dramatic and disturbing story told on one stone in the churchyard at Knarsdale, St Jude:

In memory of Robert Baxter of Farhouse
Who died on October 4th 1796 aged 56 years
All you that please these lines to read
It will cause a tender heart to bleed
I murdered was upon the fell
And by the man I knew full well
By bread and butter which hen laid
I being harmless was betray'd
I hope he will rewarded be
That laid the poison there for me.

In Bedlington churchyard there are at least two sad tales of shipwreck; one stone shows a simply-carved upturned boat. One monument at Heddon even preserves a last will and testament. Almost every churchyard with stones of the eighteenth and early nineteenth centuries has a wealth of stories to tell. Amongst them, however, there are also many more rather dull accounts of sometimes implausible piety.

In the nineteenth century, piety gains the upper hand and inscriptions become both more prosaic and again more formulaic, reflecting the orthodox spirituality of the second half of Mrs Alexander's hymn. The stones, ever larger and more protective of jealously guarded personal space, are in the new Victorian Gothic style and whilst a few show the angel of the resurrection, complete with trumpet, most seem shy of such pictorial imagery and remain content with the simplicity of the intertwined letters I H S, either the beginning of the Greek spelling of 'Jesus' or when also intertwined with the cross an abbreviation of the Latin '*In Hoc Salus*' ('In this [cross is] salvation'). The idea of remembrance gains strength. Many stones begin 'Sacred to the memory of …' The gentler form, 'In loving memory', normally comes later. Ever more eclectic influences can be seen on later nineteenth-century grave-stones, as well as the effect of new artistic movements, but, especially after the First World War, there is a marked move away from ostentation towards a new simplicity.

Victorian hope in the resurrection gives way in the twentieth century to simpler expres-sions of personal and private grief. Regional styles not only continue to show the preferences of individual stonemasons but also national trends in attitudes to death and whatever may lie beyond it. Although more personal, epitaphs remained formulaic and conformist.

We have now come a long way from the stark confrontation with death of the early eighteenth century and have even moved away from the conventional piety and hope in the resurrection of Mrs Alexander and her contemporaries. As death has become more and more remote from our sight and experience, and as cremation has also become the norm by which most people now choose to dispose of their dead, popular attitudes to death, seen both in funeral tributes and on gravestones, have changed too. There is now an almost contradic-tory process of de-emphasising the reality of decay and the harshness of separation. 'Death is nothing at all …' for the many people who stress instead the continuity of the self beyond this life. Gravestones bear photographs of the living and images of an open door to heaven.

My intention has not been to criticise this or any other view, but simply to record its effect on the way we mark death and on the physical reminders of that in our remaining 'open' churchyards.[4] Some may find it perhaps not a little ironic that in a time when the Church itself seems now less sure and certainly less united in its understanding of the meaning of life and death it is still concerned to define the kind of text and which images on grave memori-als count as good taste – and what lies beyond the pale. Churchyards are part of our heritage, but, just like church buildings, they have evolved over many years and have changed often. How that change is to be most effectively managed is an open and intriguing question.

EIGHT

BELLS IN THE DIOCESE OF NEWCASTLE

HOWARD SMITH

Bells pronounce the Gospel of good news to everyone. They call the faithful to church week by week and ring out on joyful occasions such as baptisms and weddings. They announce glad tidings for the nation. They toll to summon us to the grave and to the life eternal.

A bell does not sound a single note. It is made up of many identifiable notes that come from different areas of the bell with different lengths of audibility. It may sound relatively pleasing and in tune even though these partial tones are not strictly in tune with one another.

Many churches began with one bell, tuned to no specific note. If a second bell was purchased, the church had to decide if this was to be larger, with a deeper note, or smaller, with a higher note. If a third bell was obtained, matters swiftly became more complicated. It is often the case that the harmonics or 'overtones' of two or three old bells can clash with each other and sound quite painful to the listener. When extra bells were obtained it was sometimes the practice not to use bells together but to use them singly and for specific purposes. For example, there might be a curfew bell, a 'soul' or 'passing' bell, a 'pancake' bell, an 'angelus' bell and a 'fray' or warning bell (warning bells were common in troubled border parishes).

It is now possible to tune new bells very accurately. There are two major bell foundries in England: Taylor, Eayre and Smith of Loughborough and the Whitechapel Bell Foundry in London, which has been in existence for over 500 years.

There are a number of different ways by which a bell can be made to sound:

'Clocking', when the clapper inside the bell is swung through a small arc to hit the inside of the bell but the bell itself does not move.

'Chiming', when a chiming hammer, not connected to the bell, moves a very small distance to strike the bell, (either on the inside or outside of the sound bow) and then drops away. (One person can comfortably chime a large number of bells by means of an 'Ellacombe Chiming Apparatus'.)

'Swing Chiming', when the bell swings through a relatively small arc and the clapper inside it strikes the bell during its swing.

'Ringing', when the bell swings through an arc greater than 360 degrees and then fully back again – sometimes called 'full circle ringing'. Very slow full circle ringing, as at a funeral, is known as 'tolling'.

If the bells are rung in a numerical order, with the treble (the highest note and lightest bell) first and the tenor (the heaviest and deepest note) last, it is known as 'ringing rounds'. There are many computations in the order that bells can be sounded. 'Change ringing' describes an often complex mathematical pattern of full circle ringing.

In a tower with three bells there are six different sequential changes that can be rung: 123 – 213 – 231 – 321 – 312 – 132 – 123; or alternatively the reverse: 123 – 132 – 312 – 321 – 231 – 213 – 123 .

NUMBER OF BELLS	POSSIBLE CHANGES	TIME TAKEN
3	6	quarter of a minute
4	24	one minute
5	120	five minutes
6	720	thirty minutes
7	5040	three hours
8	40320	all day!

A 'peal' is continuous ringing of at least 5000 different changes which might last about three hours. Peals are often rung for special occasions. The heavy weight of the bells at Newcastle Cathedral means that a peal using twelve bells usually lasts about three and a half hours.

Bells are normally rung by full circle to change ringing in the following places in the diocese – not all are churches:

Rings of 13	Newcastle Cathedral
Rings of 10	Gosforth, All Saints
	Hexham Abbey
	Christ Church, North Shields
Rings of 8	Allendale, St Cuthbert
	Bamburgh, St Aidan
	Berwick-upon-Tweed Town Hall
	Fenham, St James and St Basil
	Low Elswick, St Stephen
	Morpeth Watch Tower[1]
	Newcastle, St George
	Newcastle, St John the Baptist
	Newcastle, St Matthew and St Mary
	Rothbury, All Saints
	Whitley Bay, St Paul
Rings of 6	Benwell, St James
	Cramlington, St Nicholas
	Embleton, Holy Trinity
	Newton Hall, Mowden School Chapel
	Ponteland, St Mary
	Wylam, St Oswin[2]

A number of churches also own a set of handbells. These can be used to play tunes as well as to imitate change ringing.

The largest bell in the diocese, the 'Major', is at Newcastle Cathedral and chimes the hours. It is 83.5in in diameter and was cast in 1891 by Taylor's of Loughborough. It weighs a staggering 5 tons, 18 hundredweight and 2 quarters, (approximately 6,019 kilos). It replaced the original 'Major' cast by Sir R.S. Hawks and Co. of Gateshead. Newcastle Cathedral has the only ring of 13 bells in the diocese. The heaviest of the ringing bells is almost 2 tons. There are also three medieval bells, one of which is chimed by the Verger as a service bell. There are at least 26 bells over 500 years old in the diocese including, at Mitford, one that was cast no later than about 1150.

There were once other local foundries. Three bells cast in 1878 by the Newcastle firm Cox and Sons are at Warden Church. Seven bells remain which were cast by John Lee of Newcastle between 1737-68. Between 1864-8 John Mills and Co. of Newcastle cast three bells, which also remain.[3] Thirty bells were made for churches in the diocese by the Watson family of High Bridge in Newcastle between 1811-78, but all are now lost.[4]

In 1539, as part of the Dissolution of the Monasteries, the Commissioners of King Henry VIII removed the six bells from the central tower of Tynemouth Priory. They were taken to London and probably melted down to cast cannon for the King's Army or Navy.

The only foreign bells are an American example at Lambley and one from the Low Countries at Eglingham.

NINE

MUSIC IN THE DIOCESE OF NEWCASTLE: A PERSONAL APPRECIATION

JOHN ROPER

Craftsman's art and music's measure
for Thy pleasure
all combine

Thus says Francis Pott (1832-1909) in his famous hymn 'Angel-voices ever singing', a hymn so evocative of the hosts of heaven making music round God's throne and for God's pleasure.

I believe that although there are many styles of church music, visitors to our churches somehow expect to hear an organ playing in the background and, probably more in the expectation of their imaginations, a choir singing plainsong chants or ethereal versions of *Miserere*. So, I look first at organs and their part in the worship of our churches.[1]

Church musicians are leaders but not solo performers. There are often musicians in churches throughout the country who fail at the first while being gifted exponents of the second; as music forms such an integral part of worship, the results of both are unsatisfactory and fail our congregations. After all, music is a ministry in the Church, and the leadership of organists, musicians and choirs is essential to help inspire our congregations in their shared worship of God. I do not believe it is appropriate simply to accept uninspiring or overbearing music, as this may so easily lead to lacklustre worship.

Another common and recurring problem, especially in the more rural areas of Northumberland, is the lowly position organs sometimes have on church-maintenance priorities lists, despite the fact that the organ is likely to be the most expensive item in the building. Perhaps this is an unavoidable fact of church financial life, but on more than one occasion tuners have been called in emergencies to failing organs, almost inevitably at a higher cost than an annual maintenance contract!

Many organs, especially in rural areas, are small, but, in most cases, suit the buildings in which they are housed and meet the needs of the regular worshipping congregations. Some churches have invested in electronic digital organs – from one-manual instruments to much larger ones. Many organs also have an interesting history and possess unique features.

There are two rural church organs, known to me personally, that are clear examples of this. The first, in the village church of Hunstanworth, St James, is a little gem of an organ, built reputedly for the Great Exhibition in 1851 by Gray and Davison. It has only two

stops and is hand-pumped, but has a most attractive Victorian case, with highly decorative painted pipe-work. The second is in the church of St Mungo, Simonburn. This
was built by J. W. Walker and Sons at the turn of the nineteenth and twentieth centuries
and was used in York Minster while the Minster organ was undergoing renovation. It was
purchased by Simonburn Church and erected there in May 1903 and was overhauled in
1955. In 1991, Harrison and Harrison of Durham refurbished the instrument and it is now
once again in the care of J. W. Walker and Sons. It has two keyboards and pedals, boasts
two very satisfactory divisions (Great and Swell) and has been recorded on a number of
occasions.

   The city of Newcastle can, of course, boast a number of fine instruments, not least the
organ in St Nicholas Cathedral (originally built by Harris (the elder) in 1676, with its last
rebuild undertaken by Nicholson & Co. of Worcester in 1981); and Hexham Abbey houses
a fine Phelps organ, built in 1974 as part of the church's 1300th anniversary of the found-
ing of the abbey by St Wilfrid. Also worth noting is the T. C. Lewis and Co. (1885) organ at
Cullercoats, St George which has an Historic Organs Certificate, awarded by the British
Institute of Organ Studies.[2]

   Unfortunately, there are a dwindling number of choirs that maintain the Anglican choral
tradition. This is a shame. A choir's leadership can greatly encourage congregations and give a
lift to worship. As with all the music in liturgy, dull or poor singing can prove to be uninspiring
and detrimental, so it is important that choirs can uplift and move congregations in a positive
way. There are, however, an encouraging number of places, which, often making imaginative
use of limited resources, seek to blend the best of traditional and contemporary music. Special
mention in the diocese should be made of the rich musical life and fine choirs at the cathedral
and at Hexham Abbey. Some choirs mix young and adult voices, others rely mainly on adults.

   Generally speaking, however, the music at parish level should be kept simple and well
led rather than be too difficult and badly executed! There is much fine music available to
all parishes other than just hymns and psalms, including some splendid Eucharist settings,
designed for congregational participation, and new songs, hymns and chants from the Taizé
and Iona communities. One happy consequence of the Iona tradition has been a rediscovery
of singing unaccompanied. At least one parish, Newcastle, St John, maintains the old 'west
gallery' tradition of instruments to accompany congregational singing. Many other churches,
including Hexham Abbey, have encouraged highly skilled music groups to lead worship
– especially in more contemporary styles.

   The Royal School of Church Music in Northumbria, through its outreach programme
and regular choir festivals, encourages many groups to come together to sing those things
which otherwise might be beyond their scope. Some of the new music to which I have
alluded can also be introduced through these gatherings.

   Churches play an important role as a focus of music in the community. It is important
for the lives of people, especially in rural areas perhaps, to be able to hear and appreciate
music and art outside the liturgical setting. Many churches regularly serve as a venue for
concerts and host a number of music groups and societies throughout the year. Some parishes enjoy special links with local schools. There are also the important music festivals at
Hexham Abbey each September and the Brinkburn Priory Summer Music Festival, which
both combine music from around the world with the very best of music and art by local and
national groups and musicians.

   Finally, I return to Francis Pott and his clear and striking vision of heavenly music. Larry
Ellis says, in an essay entitled 'My vision in the Ministry of Worship and Music':

> The musical style within a particular church will generally be a reflection of personal tastes that are present within that church. I believe as ministers of music we are stewards of God's music, not curators ….We must stimulate and create opportunities for all to share the gifts of music …. Any time the attention is drawn more to the performer than to God, the musician has done a great injustice.

Above all, we must not forget that our sacrifice of praise (as F.S. Pierpoint puts it in his hymn *For the beauty of the earth*), through music and singing, is demanded by God. It is not an option! In 1 Chronicles 16, we are commanded to 'Sing unto the Lord, all the earth! … Ascribe unto the Lord the glory due unto his name!' and, in Psalm 66, the psalmist states we should 'Make a joyful noise to God all the earth; sing the glory of his name; give to him glorious praise!' The psalmist also encourages us to 'Sing praises to the Lord with the lyre … with trumpets and the sound of the horn make a joyful noise before the King!' (Psalm 98), to which we could add 'Lute and harp … strings and pipe … loud crashing cymbals' (Psalm 150).

And Paul, writing to the Ephesians, says (in chapter 6): 'But be filled with the Spirit, addressing one another in psalms and hymns and spiritual songs, singing and making melody to the Lord with all your heart, always and for everything giving thanks in the name of our Lord Jesus Christ to God the Father'.

> Craftsman's art and music's measure
> for Thy pleasure
> all combine.

TEN

GAZETTEER

INTRODUCTION: HELEN SAVAGE

This is a brief guide to each Anglican place of worship in the Diocese of Newcastle. It is organised alphabetically by place and by 12 local 'deaneries' – the pastoral and administrative units used by the Church of England today. At the end there are brief notes about a few churches of special architectural merit now not used regularly, or at all, for worship. There are, of course, also a number of Roman Catholic and Non-conformist places of worship that are of considerable architectural or historical interest. Many of these are described in detail by Pevsner.[1]

Since the diocese first published its *Guide to the Anglican Churches in Newcastle and Northumberland* in 1982[2] (to mark the centenary of the creation of the diocese) three new places of worship have been built: North Gosforth, St Columba (in the mid-1980s), Kingston Park, St John (1991) and Byker, St Martin (2006), and at least 20 have closed for a number of reasons. In addition a significant number of churches have been restored and altered, often to enable them to be used more effectively throughout the week to serve the wider communities in which they are set. A good example of this is Tynemouth, St John Percy and Peter Robinson's chapter lists a number of other reordering projects of note.

Such changes should be no surprise. The story told throughout this gazetteer is one of change, often on a radical scale and with an apparent lack of sensitivity as judged by the conservation standards taken for granted today. The simple truth is that buildings demand constant maintenance (which is not always made easier when they are caught up in border skirmishes or used as a gun battery – as was the fate of the tower at Newburn in 1640). The sad fact is that many Northumberland churches were not well maintained and very few saw building work in the fourteenth and fifteenth centuries because of a number of factors of which the instability of the whole border region is the most significant. In this respect, the churches of the Newcastle Diocese are strikingly dissimilar to those of more settled dioceses further south. Apart from the very notable exceptions of Morpeth, St Mary, St Nicholas Cathedral, Alnwick, St Michael and Newcastle, St John, the high medieval period is largely notable for the absence of church building.

A quick glance at the gazetteer will show that there was a great deal of building activity in the relatively settled and prosperous twelfth and thirteenth centuries, but, though these buildings may have replaced earlier ones, it would be a mistake to assume that the first churches of the region were built in wood. Wherever there is evidence of early building (and the diocese is particularly rich in Saxon architecture) it is in stone. No Saxon church survives intact, but the finest example is undoubtedly at Corbridge, with a string of others in the Tyne Valley including Heddon-on-the-Wall, Ovingham, Bywell, St Andrew, Warden and Hexham Abbey (the superb crypt). Saxon building can also be seen further north in a number of rural churches including Bolam, Hartburn and Whittingham. There is strong evidence of Saxon work in many others.

No twelfth or thirteenth-century church in the diocese remained unaltered by later builders. Perhaps the most striking example of a church from this period is Warkworth, but Brinkburn Abbey, Hexham, Norham, Newcastle, St Andrew, Haltwhistle, Ponteland, Ovingham, Bywell, St Peter, Felton, Bolam, Hartburn and Whalton are amongst other notable survivals. They represent a high point in early medieval church building in the region. As Simon Jenkins says:

> Above all, Northumberland is uniquely a county of early Gothic …. The characteristic soaring lancet beneath a steep gable is best displayed on a small scale at Ovingham and Corbridge, but few churches in the north of England equal the spectacular interior and monastic relics of Hexham.[3]

One church from the seventeenth century, Berwick, Holy Trinity (1650-52), is worthy of special note – it is the only parish church built during the English Commonwealth. Less imposing work from the sixteenth and seventeenth centuries may be seen in the simple beauty of the little church of Halton, near Corbridge. New building was rare in the eighteenth century, repair being more the order of the day, but Newcastle, St Ann and Newcastle, All Saints are notable exceptions. Tynemouth (North Shields), Christ Church is also a substantially eighteenth-century building, although it incorporates both seventeenth and nineteenth-century work.

Churches have generally been rebuilt because their congregations aspire to the best contemporary standards (which is why there are few Saxon churches in the most prosperous parts of the country where the grandest medieval buildings are also found) – or else, as was the sad fate of many of our churches, it was out of dire necessity. We may not always admire the way in which the Victorians 'restored' almost every medieval church in the region, but the story told here is that in very many cases such wholesale rebuilding often followed earlier attempts, often in the eighteenth century, to carry out emergency repairs.

Major repairs to almost every ancient church in the diocese were carried out during the nineteenth century. Later in the century, the number of new builds gathered pace around the time of, and just after, the foundation of the diocese in 1882. Some of these new churches are very fine indeed. The names of around a dozen nineteenth-century architects occur again and again through the gazetteer. Best-known is John Dobson, whose Newcastle churches of St Thomas and Jesmond, Clayton Memorial (Jesmond Parish Church), built at either end of his long career, illustrate his ability to work in markedly different styles. This facility is clearly reflected in the huge number of alterations, restorations and rebuilds he carried out throughout the diocese. W. S. Hicks was almost as prolific, and some of the finest work in the latter part of the century was done by R. J. Johnson, notably in St Nicholas Cathedral but also in the new churches of Newcastle, St Matthew and St Mary, Gosforth, All Saints and Wylam. Two of the most impressive late nineteenth-century churches are, however, the sole ecclesiastical examples of the work of architects in the diocese: Cullercoats, St George, by J.L. Pearson and then Newcastle (Jesmond), St George, by Thomas Spence (otherwise a shipyard architect!).

The twentieth century saw the very particular Fenham, St James and St Basil (1927-31) built in the Arts and Crafts style by Eric Lofting. It is the last large church in the diocese to have been built in stone. Brick (albeit old brick in the case of Fenham, Holy Cross, built just a few years later) has been the main medium since. Utmost simplicity, low cost, speed of construction and multi-purpose use characterise most of the outer suburban churches of the 1950s and early 1960s. Since then, the few new churches to be built have demonstrated a little more flair, but the need for adaptability has remained.

For centuries churches have stood at the heart of our communities and have been used for a multiplicity of functions. It is thoroughly in keeping with this ancient tradition that so many buildings are now being adapted to more open community use.

The gazetteer has been compiled from a number of sources. In most instances, the primary material has been supplied by the parishes themselves and includes information gleaned from a growing number of parish websites, some of which are very detailed. The main diocesan website provides links to all of them.[4] In a few cases the 1982 *Guide* has been invaluable, but by far the best and most carefully researched account of the buildings of Northumberland (including Newcastle) is that by Sir Nikolaus Pevsner, which in its 1992 revision incorporates the observations of a number of leading scholars based in the region. In the few cases where there has been a major discrepancy between the information gathered from the parishes and that in Pevsner we have (mostly, though not quite always) followed Pevsner. Short of an exhaustive architectural and historical study of each building, way beyond the scope of this present book, it is not possible to corroborate or comment authoritatively on all the information or dates we copy here, but we hope that in the vast majority of cases the guide will prove trustworthy.

Pevsner supplies a full and fascinating glossary of architectural terms. We also felt that it would be helpful to include a very brief glossary here. You can find it at the end of the gazetteer.

One of the delights of Pevsner is that he offers often trenchant criticism (and equally lavish praise) of the buildings he observes. In this we have not felt it right to try to follow his lead, though we have noted some of his comments in passing. The purpose of the gazetteer is to give brief and, we hope, readable information about the churches we care for and of which we are proud. We hope you find it interesting and that it will inspire you to visit many of the buildings listed here and to enjoy them in the context of town and landscape, history, tradition and culture. For as Jenkins points out:

> This is more a county of churches in their settings, of black stone, blowing trees and Roman and Saxon carvings. Like Cornwall this is England at its extremes.[5]

CLASSIFICATION OF CHURCHES IN THE DIOCESE

GRADE	NUMBER OF CHURCHES
Grade I	39
Grade II*	23
Grade II	85
Unlisted	99
Total	246

BEDLINGTON DEANERY

Bedlington, St Cuthbert

Saxon features may survive at St Cuthbert's – a small window beside the pulpit, the imposing
doorway in the same south wall and a stone carving of two figures. The chancel arch, with its
Romanesque 'dog tooth' decoration, is probably twelfth-century but was altered later, perhaps
in the fifteenth century. A south porch was added in the fourteenth century (now the memorial chapel) and the trefoil squint to the left of the chancel arch was opened. In 1817 the north
wall of the church was pulled down and a huge semi-circular structure with galleries was built.
The chancel was rebuilt in 1847 and the rather forbidding tower in 1868. In 1912 the semi-
circular structure was replaced by a huge 'aisle', along with a suite of vestries and new windows
in the south wall. In June 2002 a new stone floor was laid in the nave. The aisle was divided off
to make a 'community space' and a small chapel, and in 2004 the fine two-manual Nicholson
organ of 1877 was rebuilt and restored to a new west gallery.

Several twelfth- to fourteenth-century grave-covers are set in the south and west walls of
the nave. The most interesting glass is perhaps that of the west window of the aisle. It displays,
as Pevsner remarks: 'a strange mixture' of Christian and Masonic imagery.

When the monks of Durham fled carrying the body of Cuthbert ahead of the advance
north of William the Conqueror, they are said to have found shelter in Bedlington Church
on 12 December 1069.

A small stone marks the sad death of Cuthbert Watson who fell from the tower while
sleepwalking on 14 February 1669.

Michael Longridge who owned the famous Bedlington Iron and Engine Works is buried
in the churchyard.

Blyth, St Cuthbert

The present Victorian Gothic church, begun in 1884 to a design by W.S. Hicks, replaced a chapel of ease built in 1751. The baptistry, vestries, vestibule and porch were added in 1891 and in the following year the tower and transepts were completed. When the tower was first built it was adorned with stone pinnacles and a weathercock, but these were removed after one was blown off and damaged the roof of the nave in a winter gale in 1937. The window over the high altar '*The Crucifixion*' is in memory of Dr Henry Ward who died in 1891. The clock tower was presented by Mr G. Colpitts in memory of his wife in 1962. The west window '*The Four Works of Mercy*' was a memorial to Dr Gilbert Ward. In 2003 the bells were completely refurbished and the new windows in the chapel were given by Mrs Holgeth.

Blyth, St Mary

The chancel, nave and south porch were built by Austin and Johnson as a chapel of ease in 1864 in thirteenth and fourteenth-century style. The north aisle and extensions to the chancel and west end by W.S. Hicks were added between 1897 and 1902 following the formation of the parish. The 1936 font was brought from the redundant church of St Lawrence, Byker in 1979. The east window is by Atkinson Brothers (1911) and the north aisle window is by Leonard Evetts (1950).

The large crucifix outside the church came from a London church bombed in the Second World War.

Burradon, The Good Shepherd

The Church of the Good Shepherd was built as a mission chapel in 1894 using locally quarried freestone. It was renovated during the 1960s when a toilet and wash room were added. The imposing cross outside the church at the entrance to Kirkwood Estate is hewn from Australian hardwood, salvaged from Burradon Colliery. It was dedicated on 22 January 1979.

Cambois, St Andrew

St Andrew's has been described as 'a (much-loved) brick box with a fleche!' It was consecrated in 1898. The choir stalls were removed and the organ was moved to the back in about 1960.

Choppington, St Paul the Apostle

A small, unpretentious stone-built colliery church, consecrated in 1866 and set in an unusually large churchyard.

Cowpen, St Benedict

A simple brick structure, consecrated in 1961.

Cramlington, St Nicholas

A chapel existed at Cramlington from 1270. The present church is said to have been adapted from a design by John Dobson by Austin and Johnson and was built in 1868 by Waterston and Stafford of Morpeth at a cost of £3000. It incorporates two stained-glass windows by Cottier. The altar is of black oak from the Blyth Valley. The stone font is inlaid with coloured marble and there are notable carvings on the reredos, over the altar, on the lectern (a spread eagle, by Bulletti of Newcastle) and on the pulpit (by Stafford of Morpeth). The organ, by Nicholson of Newcastle, was installed later at a cost of £165. The rood screen was installed in 1895.

When the church was consecrated and dedicated by the Bishop of Durham on 12 May 1868, 630 people were present for the service and the villagers of Cramlington all took a holiday.

Delaval, Our Lady

A blocked window on the outside of the north wall of the nave suggests a Saxon origin, as does the font, but this beautiful little church is said to have been built as a private chapel by Hubert (or Guy) de Laval in 1102 (the nephew by marriage of William the Conqueror) and consecrated by Bishop Flambard of Durham. It retains many distinctive Romanesque architectural features with decorative moulding (especially on the two arches which divide the nave, choir and a separate sanctuary). A Romanesque or possibly fourteenth-century piscina can also still be seen.

There is a very fine early fourteenth-century effigy of a knight, perhaps Sir Hugh Delaval, and a slightly later one of a lady; eight cusped panels containing shields bearing Delaval and other arms from the fourteenth century; six eighteenth- and nineteenth-century funeral hatchments of later Delaval and Hastings families, and a fine eighteenth-century ceiling in the nave. The east window, a copy of an early fourteenth-century three-light window, was replaced in 1861. The other lancet windows are all also nineteenth-century. A porch was added in 1895, above which is a window carved from one stone, thought to be originally part of a fourteenth-century east window.

Dudley, St Paul

The decision to build a mission church at Dudley was made in 1883. The small stone building was completed in May 1886 and dedicated on 14 December that year. A hall was added in 1912. Much of the original dark wood furnishing was replaced in 1966. The organ (by Nicholson) was installed in 1935. A memorial to those who had worked in the Dudley Pit was placed in the church when the colliery closed in 1977.

Holywell, St Mary

Originally a chapel of ease, St Mary's is a simple half-timbered structure built to a design by W.S. Hicks and consecrated in 1885. Pevsner rightly calls it 'pretty' and admires the clever construction of the bellcote at the west end.

Horton, St Mary the Virgin

Horton Church is first recorded in 1147. A twelfth-century tympanum is preserved above the south door. The present building was built in 1827, but incorporates a slightly earlier transept. It was restored and 'Gothicized' in 1903 by Hicks when the south porch was also added.

The building incorporates an eighteenth-century sundial, the bell dates from 1621 and a tombstone of 1517 (of Anne Harbottle) is set in the outside of the south wall.

Killingworth, St John the Evangelist

Designed by E. Bassett Keeling of London, this rather fine mid-Victorian Gothic church is faced in local stone, with decorative bands of red sandstone, also from a nearby quarry. The two-manual tracker organ was installed when the church was built in 1869, but bought second-hand!

New Hartley, St Michael and All Angels

The present red-brick building with stone capping replaced a small nineteenth-century wooden church and was built in 1900 to a design by J. Dobinson of the Seaton Delaval Coal Company.

Newsham, St Bede

The hall (once the church) and vicarage were built in 1930 to a distinctive design with Dutch gable ends by Charlewood of Newcastle. The church, the fourth since 1892, was designed in a more modern style by the same architect in 1957. The altar is of a very solid stone construction against the east wall. The pews are of finely turned oak.

Seaton Sluice, St Paul

A simple structure, formerly a community hall, conse-crated as a church in 1961.

Seghill, Holy Trinity

A simple stone church designed by John and Benjamin Green and opened in 1849. The hall was added in 1981.

Sleekburn, St John
(Bedlington Station)

St John's was designed by Arthur Plummer in early 'Perpendicular' style and opened in 1906. The exterior is of local colliery brick. Inside, there are stone arcades and facings, a mosaic chancel pavement by Emley of Newcastle, pulpit and chancel stalls of carved oak by Ralph Hedley and glazing by Atkinson's of Newcastle.

Stakeford, Holy Family

A simple dual-purpose, brick-built hall, opened in 1962.

BELLINGHAM DEANERY

Bellingham, St Cuthbert

The present church was built in the twelfth or early thirteenth century and probably replaced a still older building. The medieval church had a choir and a nave of four bays, with narrow aisles on each side. The stump ends of the springers of the arcades can still be seen protruding inside at each end of the nave. A south-aisle transept was also added later in the thirteenth century. By 1609 the building was a roofless ruin. During the seventeenth century the present vaulted stone ceilings of the south transept and nave were built. These are of Roman vault slabs laid on heavy ribs. Such a stone roof is enormously heavy and in the eighteenth century external buttresses had to be added to the nave. After 1843 the roofs of the choir and nave/south transept were replaced and repaired. Two more buttresses were built against the west gable and a west window was added. In about 1885 floor tiles and pews were fitted, central heating was installed and the south doorway was blocked. In 1960 the choir stalls were removed, a new altar rail was installed and the organ (built by Binns of Leeds in 1926 and restored in 1996) was moved to its present position in the south transept.

The post-Reformation font, an octagonal stone pillar, has a wooden carved lid with metal circlet inscribed in memory of Bellingham men who died in the Second World War.

Three cannon balls were found during the work on the nave and south transept roofs after 1843.

In the churchyard, the Long (Lang) Pack tomb on the north side of the church is associated with a gruesome murder in 1723.

St Cuthbert performed a miracle at Bellingham. He also found and then consecrated 'Cuddy's Well'.

Bingfield, St Mary

A simple stone church, which incorporates some medieval stone but dates mostly to restorations in the early eighteenth century (the bellcote and south doorway) and to 1875.

Birtley, St Giles

A small seventh-century memorial stone, now set in the chancel wall, is evidence of a very early church here. The present solid stone church has a Romanesque chancel arch. There is a blocked sixteenth-century doorway in the north wall of the nave. St Giles was restored and partly rebuilt in 1884.

Several medieval gravestones now stand in the porch. An unusual three-sided gravestone can be found in the churchyard.

Byrness, St Francis

This tiny stone-built chapel is dated (on the inner door) 1796 and was consecrated three years later. The chancel was partially rebuilt in 1884 and the interior remodelled. A remarkable window installed in 1903 commemorates those who died during the construction of the Catcleugh reservoir. As Pevsner notes, it even includes an illustration of a narrow-gauge steam railway.

Byrness St Francis

Chollerton, St Giles

The present church is said to have been built in about 1260 by William de Swinburne, a Scottish knight who replaced an earlier building. It makes use of Roman stone probably from the nearby fort at Chesters, including whole pillars that now form the south arcade, which was raised in the mid-twelfth century. The north arcade has fourteenth-century octagonal piers. St Giles's was extensively altered in the mid-eighteenth century and again in 1873 when the wood-shingled spire was built.

There are two fonts. One is a substantial Roman altar, turned upside down. It was dedicated to Jupiter and was found buried in the churchyard in 1827. The other is thirteenth-century. The organ, given to the church in about 1850, is said to contain work by 'Father' Schmidt – the famous seventeenth-century organ-builder.

An early gravestone built into the wall of the porch may be of Elizabeth, the wife of William de Swinburne.

Corsenside, St Cuthbert

Corsenside is traditionally one of four places to which the monks of Lindisfarne bore St Cuthbert's body around 875, but a cross-base and possible sections of wayside crosses are the only evidence of an early church. The plain chancel arch is the only surviving architectural feature of a Romanesque two-cell church. The walls were heightened in the seventeenth century and a priest's door was added or altered at about the same time. The south window in the chancel, bellcote and south door were added around 1735, when the font and communion rails were probably installed. The annex and porch at the west end and the nave windows are perhaps of the mid-nineteenth century. Most of the wooden furnishings date to an internal restoration in 1914, when the medieval slabs were also brought inside the church.

The chancel arch is flanked by early nineteenth-century Commandment boards and there are three slots in each side for a rood screen.

The tall limestone octagonal eighteenth-century font is of two parts (bowl and stem) set in a stone base; the stones may originally have been parts of a wayside cross.

Elsdon, St Cuthbert

Pevsner describes St Cuthbert's as 'a church with a complex history; it was once larger than it is'. A blocked tower arch may be twelfth-century, as are the western responds of the arcade. Two early thirteenth-century lancet windows may also have formed part of the early larger church, which seems to have been largely rebuilt in the fourteenth century. The unusual aisles are very narrow with rare quadrant vaulted roofs. Pevsner suggests that they may date to the sixteenth or early seventeenth century, and with their thick outer walls may have been partly a defensive feature. The chunky bellcote was added in about 1720. During the nineteenth century the church was restored twice – in 1837, when the south porch was added, and then again in 1877.

Several medieval grave-slabs have been placed in the church, as well as a fragment of an inscription from the Roman outpost fort at Risingham and a gabled tombstone from the next fort north along Dere Street at High Rochester.

Falstone, St Peter

A pre-Reformation chapel existed at Falstone by 1541. It was restored and used for a short time in the early eighteenth century as a Presbyterian chapel. A new Anglican chapel was built in 1824–5 by John and Benjamin Green but burned down in 1890 and was restored in 1891 by Plummer and Burrell. It is in Perpendicular style with a western tower. A new organ was installed in 1998.

Small fragments of at least two different early medieval (perhaps ninth-century) crosses were found at various times at local sites. An unusual early eighteenth-century gravestone shows a 'dance of death' – a little girl holding hands with a skeleton.

Gunnerton, St Christopher

A simple rough-faced stone church built in 1899 and consecrated the following year. The architect was John Hawes. The west gallery includes fine 'Arts and Crafts' style carving.

Heavenfield (St Oswald in Lee)

The present stone church was built in 1737 to replace an earlier building of unknown date (a decorated twelfth-century corbel stone is built into the north wall). It was remodelled and 'gothicized' by W.S. Hicks in 1887. A Roman altar inside the church has been reused as a cross base.

The church is said to be on the site of the Battle of Heavenfield where, in 634, King Oswald of Northumbria defeated the pagan Cadwallon. There is no clear evidence that the church itself has Saxon origins, though this has been suggested.

Horsley, Holy Trinity

Holy Trinity was designed for Lord Redesdale by John and Benjamin Green in neo-Norman style as a chapel of ease. It was consecrated in 1844. The organ and western gallery were added in 1997 and the entrance remodelled.

There is a Roman altar in the porch.

Humshaugh, St Peter

St Peter's was designed by H.H. Seward and built by Thomas Nixon of Wark in 1818 to replace a ruined chapel at Haughton Castle. The building is of hand-dressed freestone. The sanctuary was reordered in about 1925. The windows include the arms of King George III and of the Greenwich Hospital. The two-manual organ is by Bishop and Son (1920). There is a window (in the south wall of the nave) by Kempe made in the early years of the twentieth century.

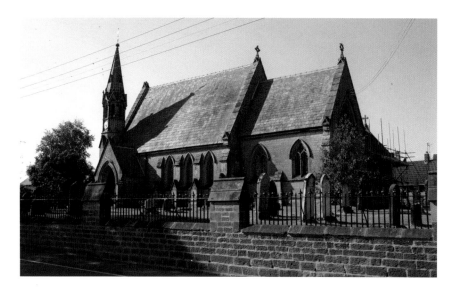

Otterburn, St John the Evangelist

St John's, the work of John Dobson, was built in Decorated style in 1858 and then altered in 1910 and 1932. As well as some good Victorian glass there are windows by Evetts (1966 and 1977). The organ (1910) by Nicholson and Newbegin was the gift of Sir Charles and Lady Morrison-Bell who also donated the elaborately carved Italian altar.

Simonburn, St Mungo

Until the early nineteenth century St Mungo's was one of the largest parishes in England, and covered about 260 square miles of the North Tyne Valley. The church has Saxon roots, but only a few fragments of sculpture remain. The present building is thirteenth-century and has a characteristically long Northumbrian chancel. It was rebuilt and restored in 1763 by Robert and William Newton, in 1863-4 by Anthony Salvin and in 1875-7 by R.J. Johnson; an unusual thirteenth-century double piscina survives in the chancel wall as well as a priest's door of the same date.

The organ (by Walker) was acquired from York Minster in about 1901 and there is some late nineteenth-century glass by Kempe.

There are some fine stone monuments in St Mungo's, including an effigy of a former vicar, Cuthbert Ridley, who died in 1620. The splendid lych-gate was built by Johnson in 1885.

Thockrington, St Aidan

St Aidan's is said to have been built in about 1100 by the Norman family of Umfraville. The Romanesque chancel walls and vaulted roof still survive. The church was extensively restored in 1876. The large circular font is probably thirteenth-century.

Lord Beveridge, founder of the modern welfare state, is buried in the churchyard.

Thorneyburn, St Aidan

St Aidan's was built in 1818 by H.H. Seward with funding from Greenwich Hospital (a major landowner in Northumberland from 1735). Along with Humshaugh, St Peter, Wark, St Michael and Greystead, St Luke (now redundant), it was built to provide livings for naval chaplains made redundant after the Battle of Trafalgar.

Wall, St George

A small, simple stone church built in Perpendicular style by Hicks and Charlewood in 1895 and consecrated in 1897. It is orientated north–south instead of the usual east–west.

Wark, St Michael

Another of the North Tyne churches built after Trafalgar in about 1818. It replaced an earlier church which may have had Saxon origins. The only evidence now of a medieval church is a font basin. The sanctuary was reordered in the 1920s.

West Woodburn, All Saints (Corsenside)

All Saints was built in 1906-7 as the parish church to replace a mission church built nearby in 1856. A simple stone building, it has a splendid carved wooden reredos with sculptures of St Oswald and St Cuthbert, inscribed in memory of Alfred Illingworth. The wooden pulpit on a stone plinth and the wooden font lid, both with memorial inscriptions, are also very fine.

CORBRIDGE DEANERY

Blanchland, St Mary the Virgin (Blanchland Abbey)

St Mary's was founded in 1165 by a Norman baron, Walter de Bolbec, as an abbey for the austere White Canons, (properly known as the Premonstratensians – the order was founded by St Norbert at Prémontré in northern France in 1120). It was ravaged by Henry VIII and its stones later used to build Blanchland village.

It was rebuilt in 1751-2 out of the bequest of Nathaniel, Lord Crewe. Of the medieval building, the chancel is early thirteenth-century, the transept is mid-thirteenth century and the tower is also thirteenth-century with a fourteenth-century belfry stage. Fragments of glass and a few tombstones also survive. The transept aisle was built in 1854 and the east wall in 1881. The woodwork in the nave is nineteenth-century; the oak screen and pews were added in 1913.

When John Wesley preached in the churchyard in 1747 he said that: 'the little town was little more than a heap of ruins!'

Bywell, St Peter

Bywell was once a thriving market town and has two superb early churches. Some of the finest Saxon architecture in Northumberland can be seen at St Peter's and especially in the now redundant church of St Andrew's (see overleaf).

Ecgbert is said to have been consecrated Bishop of Lindisfarne at St Peter's in 802 and the north wall of the nave together with the western parts of the side wall of the chancel may have formed part of that original building, which seems to have been unusually large. There are also four Saxon windows high in the north wall of the nave, and a blocked doorway in the same wall.

Most of the present building, however, dates from the thirteenth century and the tower was added in the fourteenth century. The Early English thirteenth-century lancet windows at the east end of the chancel are particularly fine.

St Peter's was extensively restored in 1849 by Benjamin Ferrey, with, according to Pevsner, 'excessive zealousy'. The north chapel was endowed by the Neville family as a chantry in the fourteenth century, but after the Reformation it became the village school, separated by a wall from the main building. There are some fine medieval grave-slabs in the porch and elsewhere.

Corbridge, St Andrew

St Andrew's is one of the oldest and finest churches in Northumberland. Pevsner describes it as 'the most important surviving Saxon monument in Northumberland, except for Hexham crypt'.

The oldest parts of the building are the lower parts of the tower which was probably built some time before 786. A blocked doorway suggests that there may once have been another structure built onto the west of the tower. The upper parts of the tower appear to be eleventh-century.

The lower part of the tower houses the baptistry with its unique Roman arch which seems to have been brought in its entirety from the nearby Roman town at Corstopitum and incorporated into the Saxon tower. Minor additions were made in the twelfth century, notably the south doorway with its Romanesque zig-zag moulding.

During the thirteenth century the original Saxon church was opened up with arcading and enlarged with the addition of chancel, transepts and aisles. The Lady Chapel was added in the fourteenth century. More recent additions and alterations have included a Victorian reordering which involved the removal of plaster and the addition of Canadian maple satinwood pews. In 1912 a new oak altar, reredos, choir screen, choir stalls and clergy desks were added. The early part of the twentieth century also saw the addition of vestries, organ chamber and south porch. The lych-gate was built in 1920 to commemorate those who had died in the First World War.

The stained glass is mostly nineteenth century by Atkinson Brothers and William Wailes of Newcastle. By the pulpit on the east wall of the south transept there is a window in the Arts and Crafts style by James Eadie Reid portraying Dorcas (an early disciple of Jesus who became ill and died, but was raised to life again by St Peter). The window featuring St Christopher carrying a child over a river is by Leonard Evetts (1975). The most recent addition to the glass, commissioned to mark the 2000 millennium, is a piece of sculpture by Rob Robertson which symbolises Christian Corbridge. It can be found in the east window of the north transept.

The church possesses other work from the Arts and Crafts Movement, in particular a fine altar frontal.

A collection of medieval grave-slabs and crosses can also be seen inside the church. The solid stone building on the south side of the churchyard is also very unusual – a fourteenth-century vicar's pele built with reused Roman stones.

Edmundbyers, St Edmund

A church has existed here since at least the twelfth century, traces of which include the window openings on the south side of the chancel, the north wall and the south door. The 'three-decker' pulpit is eighteenth century along with the box pews, ceiling gallery and plastered walls. A further major restoration followed in the late nineteenth century by the then incumbent, Walker Featherstonehaugh.

A medieval grave cover (of a priest) is built into the porch wall. The stone altar was removed in 1571, hidden by local people, rediscovered in 1855 and restored to the chancel.

Halton, St Oswald, St Cuthbert and King Alfwald

This small church with a long dedication is said to have been built on or near the spot where Alfwald, king of Bernicia, was murdered on 23 September 788. The present building was thought to be Romanesque, but Pevsner points out that the nave quoins in the north-west corner may be Saxon. The chancel arch is Romanesque. All other features are sixteenth or early seventeenth century. The fine south door is segmental-arched and has a roll-moulded surround. It was re-roofed in 1706 with massive timbers with very short king and queen-posts. The altar table is seventeenth century and the altar rails are eighteenth century. It was restored again in 1880.

A weathered Roman altar can be seen in the churchyard (and other Roman stones have been built into the wall of the church).

Healey, St John

St John's was built in 1860 in neo-Norman style. The architect was C.E. Davis of Bath. The chancel arch is made of wood – after two attempts to erect a stone arch ended in disaster.

The tower was added in 1890 by Montgomery and Carr with a highly unusual rose window in its west wall. The three windows in the apse inserted in 1883 are the work of Baguley of Newcastle. Three windows in the nave are by Leonard Evetts, made between 1955 and 1960.

Heddon-on-the-Wall, St Andrew

St Andrew's is one of the oldest churches in Northumberland. On the outside, on the south side of the chancel, there is a blocked early Saxon doorway, and nearby where the south aisle joins the chancel, typical Saxon alternate 'long and short' work – probably a corner of the nave of the narrow Saxon building. Saxon stonework from the seventh century is claimed to be visible in the chancel wall behind the choir stalls, but Pevsner suggests that the western part of the chancel dates to some time soon after the Norman Conquest.

The church and land around Heddon were given in 1165 to the monks of Blanchland, who rebuilt the sanctuary – the east end of the chancel. Other Romanesque details from this time include the window in the north wall on the chancel. Below it is an eleventh-century grave cross. Over the years until 1392 (when the porch was built) St Andrew's was gradually extended.

New windows were inserted in the north aisle in 1839 and between 1841 and 1845 the nave was extended by the addition of a fourth bay. A new vestry was built in 1866. In the years between 1873 and 1877 a new altar, choir stalls and pulpit were introduced, as well as the organ, built by Bevington and Son of Birmingham. The glass in the east window dates from 1873 and is a 'Jesse window' – depicting Jesus's family tree in a line from Kings David and Solomon. All the other stained glass was made in 1921 – a gift of Sir James Knott, whose widow gave the pews in 1937 which came from Newcastle Cathedral.

Hunstanworth, St James

St James is a (surprisingly large for such a small community) Victorian Gothic church with a difference – its distinguished architect Samuel Sanders Teulon had French roots and he gave the building a flamboyant Burgundian patterned slate roof. It replaced a smaller medieval building and was the gift of a vicar of the parish, Daniel Capper in 1862. The hand-blown Gray and Davison organ is said to have been an exhibit in the Great Exhibition of 1851. The glass is by Kempe, Lavers and Barraud.

The First World War memorial – a wall plaque at the west end of the church – is highly unusual in that it gives thanks to God that all the men from Hunstanworth returned home safely.

Matfen, Holy Trinity

This early Victorian stone church in Early English style with single lancet windows was built by Sir Edward Blackett in 1842. The spire was added in 1853-4. The organ is the work of Nigel Church and is a gift of Ursula, Lady Blackett. The wooden lectern of 1881 is particularly fine, carved by an Italian craftsman, Bulletti, who had worked on Alnwick Castle.

Mickley, St George

St George's was built as a chapel of ease in 1825 and much extended in 1886 by W.S. Hicks, when the chancel, transepts, steeple and porch were all added in Decorated style.

Muggleswick, All Saints

The present building appears to be entirely nineteenth century, but a church was built here in the thirteenth century and replaced *c.*1728, and a dowsing survey suggests even earlier Saxon origins. Much of the furnishing was donated by the Ritson family of nearby Calf Hall.

The lych-gate is made from teak taken from HMS Powerful.

Ovingham, St Mary the Virgin

St Mary's is one of Northumberland's loveliest churches. The first building may have been built as early as the seventh century. The present tower, a magnificent example of late Saxon work and the tallest Saxon tower in the Tyne Valley, was probably erected in the late tenth or early eleventh century. The fragment of a stone cross, once built into the boilerhouse, can now be found standing beneath the pulpit. It seems to show a hunting scene from a Norse saga and was probably carved in the ninth century. Another cross fragment from this period is now in the porch along with several medieval tombstones.

Apart from the tower, most of what can now be seen at St Mary's is the result of rebuilding and expansion in the thirteenth century by powerful Norman land-owners, the Umfraville family (who also built Prudhoe Castle). The chancel and transepts, arcade and the 21 elegant lancet windows are excellent examples of the Early English architectural style in Northumberland. The outsides of the walls are supported by elegant buttresses. The alarmingly leaning wall of the south transept was given extra buttressing. The door to the vestry also dates to the thirteenth century, but the south door is a later addition. A piscina in the wall of the south transept suggests that there was originally a chantry chapel there. The church was reported to be in poor repair after the Reformation and again 300 years later. Major repairs were carried out in 1855-7 and included the renewal of the capitals on the north side of the arcade. Further major restoration was carried out during the 1990s.

Two of the three bells are medieval, probably from the fourteenth century. The organ, by Nicholson, was installed in 1880 and restored in 1981. Victorian glass is by Wailes and Strang, Baguley, Kempe and Clayton and Bell.

The famous wood engraver Thomas Bewick was born in the parish and is buried in the churchyard beside the tower.

Prudhoe, St Mary Magdalene

A simple stone church, with no aisles and short transepts built in 1880 by local subscription supported by the Duke of Northumberland.

The lych-gate serves also as Prudhoe's war memorial.

Riding Mill, St James

St James's is a splendid example of Victorian Gothic village church architecture. It was built as a chapel of ease by Mathew Thompson in 1858, largely as a result of the efforts of the Vicar of Bywell, St Andrew, the Revd J. Jaques, and became the parish church of Riding Mill in 1975. In 1879 the church was enlarged and the sanctuary and organ added. In 1963, new vestries were built in the north transept. The mosaic reredos was designed by Ada Curry in 1900.

Ryal, All Saints

The first church at Ryal was built in the twelfth century but destroyed by the Scots in 1296. It was restored only in 1878. Some Romanesque features survive, including the main doorway and the bell tower. The chancel arch is thirteenth century but with twelfth-century responds. Further restoration was carried out in 1971.

Nineteen medieval cross-slabs have been built into the west wall.

Shotley (Snod's Edge), St John

A peaceful country church, St John's was built in 1835 in imitation of early Perpendicular style. It replaced the old parish church of St Andrew, which was at Kiln Pit Hill. The chancel was added in 1903. The two bells were presented by John Leybourne, of The College, Durham, in 1835. A copy of Leonardo Da Vinci's 'Last Supper' hangs behind the altar.

Slaley, St Mary the Virgin

The present St Mary's was built in 1832, but the first church on the site is said to have been built in 1240. Most of its furnishings date from 1907-8 when it was repaired and restored. The stained-glass windows show the dates and dedications, apart from the west window, which was given by a member of the Hunting family of Slaley Hall. The pulpit is by Ralph Hedley.

The parish registers date from 1703 and record the names of several great families in the village and illustrate the occupations of parishioners, such as clogger, weaver, miller, smelter, husbandman and farmer. A kitchen and toilet were added in 1992 and in 1999 a new porch.

The lych-gate was erected in 1921 as a memorial to the fallen of the First World War.

The churchyard includes a very early headstone of 1635 (to Richard Teasdaill).

Stamfordham, St Mary

In 1848 when St Mary's was rebuilt to a design by Benjamin Ferrey he reused much of the stone from earlier churches on the site – even whole arches. Early, possibly Saxon, stone-work may be seen in the south-west corner of the nave. There is also an early blocked arch in the west wall of the tower that may be Saxon, or perhaps was built soon after the Norman Conquest. Some medieval grave monuments were also incorporated into the walls.

The 1982 *Guide* says that: 'on the chancel floor lies the sandstone body of a legless knight supposed to be Sir John De Felton who was Lord of the Matfen manor … in 1390'. What strong drink brought about poor Sir John's downfall was not recorded. There are other medieval effigies of a priest and of a knight. Nineteenth-century glass is by Kempe and Clayton and Bell.

Stocksfield, St John the Divine

St John's is a simple, rather plain church, built in 1926 as a chapel of ease to serve the rapidly growing population of Stocksfield. The porch at the west end was added in the 1950s.

Waskerley, St Matthew

A simple stone structure built as a mission church in 1898 to serve a now all but demolished railway village.

Whittonstall, St Philip and St James

Whittonstall was a chapel of ease to Bywell St Peter until 1774, when it became a parochial chapel. A fragment of an Early English capital can be seen in the porch of the present church, which was built in 1830 and reused stones from the older, possibly thirteenth-century building. The architect was Jonathon Marshall. The north wall has no windows. The chancel was added in 1896.

Wylam, St Oswin

The foundation stone of St Oswin's was laid on New Year's Day 1885. A photograph of the great day still exists – with full-bearded clergy, small boys and top-hatted gentry in the foreground, a few women and many bowler hats behind. The new church, a chapel of ease in the parish of Ovingham, was dedicated and opened on All Saints' Day 1886. The total cost, including (six) bells, organ and clock, was £7061. It was designed by R.J. Johnson, built by Scott and Son of Sunderland and paid for by George Hedley, son of William the local railway pioneer, who intended St Oswin's to be a memorial to his parents. It became a parish church in 1902.

The style of the building is Victorian Perpendicular Gothic. The tower is free-standing on three sides and its interior doubles as a south transept, now used as a chapel. The fittings and furnishings are of a high standard, with lavish use of oak. The woodwork in the chancel, including chancel screen, organ case and screen and reredos, is by Ralph Hedley (whose work also includes the rood screen and choir stalls in St Nicholas Cathedral, Newcastle). The glass in the east window is a pictorial representation of the great Latin hymn the *Te Deum*; that of the equally fine west window, installed in 1891, depicts the Last Judgement. The south porch was glazed in 1963 and the original red tiles of the entire roof were replaced in 1965 with Westmorland slate.

The lych-gate was erected in 1904.

HEXHAM DEANERY

Allendale, St Cuthbert

The present church, a Victorian Gothic building built in 1873–4, is by no means the first on the site, but for many centuries Allendale's church was dedicated not to St Cuthbert but to Our Lady. The earliest known record of a chapel is 1174. It was rebuilt in the fourteenth century and replaced by a simple structure in 1807. This was completely demolished save for a small fragment of stonework at the base of the new tower. The Victorian church was designed by Austin and Johnson; the contractors for the masonry were Peter Laing and Sons and for the woodwork the Messrs Fairlamb of Allendale. It is believed to have cost around £1500.

The alabaster and mosaic reredos depicting the Last Supper is striking.

Alston, St Augustine

The first church at Alston may have been built before the Norman Conquest, but its first appearance in the historical record does not come until the second half of the twelfth century. The medieval church was in poor repair by 1763 and was replaced six years later. This was itself wholly replaced by the present St Augustine's in 1869-70. The architect was J. W. Walton. All that remain of the earlier buildings are a stone stoup and a few decorated stones now in the church porch.

The spire, the work of G.D. Oliver, was added in 1886. The church is in Victorian Early English style with lancet and plate tracery windows. There is some attractive stained glass and a fine painted five-panel reredos depicting the Adoration of the Lamb (from the Book of Revelation). The organ, by Bryson Bros. and Ellis of London, (only one of four known to be still in use) was installed in 1878 and rebuilt in 1991. There are 10 bells in the tower, arranged as a carillon. The most remarkable feature, however, is a seventeenth-century clock and bell (now one of the 10 in the tower) that once belonged to the Earl of Derwentwater and was given to Alston church by the Commissioners of Greenwich Hospital to whom the Derwentwater estate was awarded by the Crown after the third earl's execution on a charge of treason. They were taken from Dilston Hall in 1767, but the clock was not restored until 1978.

Beltingham, St Cuthbert

The oldest part of the church probably dates from the twelfth century, but it has also been suggested that this may have been one of the places where the Lindisfarne monks rested with Cuthbert's body during their wanderings in the ninth century. A cross-slab not set in the recess of the blocked south-east door may be pre-Conquest.

The present building, a single cell structure, is predominantly late fifteenth-century with a seventeenth-century extension. It underwent a major restoration in 1884 when the vestry was also added. It was for many years a chapel of ease within Haltwhistle parish. The organ was built by Harrison and Harrison in 1905 and some glass (the east window and the west window in the north wall of the chancel) made by Kempe.

The ancient yew at Beltingham is thought to be over a thousand years old. The lych-gate was erected as a memorial to Francis Bowes-Lyon in 1904.

Fourstones, St Aidan

St Aidan's was built at the expense of the then incumbent of Warden, Mr Cruddas, as a mission church, and dedicated in 1892. It is the only wooden church in the diocese, a simple construction on a stone foundation, with a slate roof.

Garrigill, St John

Garrigill was held by the canons of Hexham Abbey from 1215 until the Dissolution in 1538. It was much rebuilt in 1790 and then much restored again in 1890. The bell was cast in about 1765. The reredos is a memorial to the fallen of the First World War.

Greenhead, St Cuthbert

St Cuthbert's was built as a chapel of ease within the parish of Haltwhistle in 1826-8 and designed by John Dobson. It was restored in 1900 when the chancel was built by Hicks and Charlewood and a spire added, along with the oak reredos and other furnishings.

Haltwhistle, Holy Cross

Soon after 1220 the Scottish crown granted land to the (Benedictine) Abbots of Arbroath to build a church for the order at Haltwhistle. Although Holy Cross was restored in 1870-1 by R.J. Johnson, it retains much of its thirteenth century, Early English character. The chancel has a piscina and trefoiled sedilia. A seventh-century water stoup suggests, however, that a much earlier church may have stood on or near the site. A local tradition has it that the stoup was used by Paulinus in his mission to convert the Northumbrians. The present font is dated 1676.

Monuments in the church include medieval grave effigies and the Ridley Memorial Stone, commemorating John, brother-in-law of the Bishop of London, Nicholas Ridley, who was burnt at the stake in Oxford in 1555 with Archbishop Thomas Cranmer.

The glass includes fine examples of the work of Morris and Co. to designs by Burne-Jones, Philip Webb and Ford Madox Brown. Other glass is by Kempe. The reredos, sculptured in marble, is very fine and depicts the Adoration of the Magi. It is a memorial to William Ives, vicar of the parish for 40 years, who died in 1875.

Haydon Bridge, St Cuthbert

St Cuthbert's was built on land donated by Greenwich Hospital in 1794 (the crest can be seen in a painting at the back of the building) and was consecrated two years later. An unusual feature is the tower roof which has an unusual pagoda-like appearance. The church was restored in 1866-9 and then enlarged in 1898-9. The stained glass includes examples by Kempe installed between 1902 and 1906 and more recently by Leonard Evetts in 1984.

Haydon Old Church

Also dedicated to St Cuthbert, this small stone church served the medieval community of Haydon, which once surrounded it. The earliest work dates from the twelfth century. A chantry was added in the fourteenth century. It was restored or repaired in about 1654 and again by C.C. Hodges in 1882/3 to enable it to be used during the summer. It still has no electricity! The altar is made of reused Roman stones and the font is carved from a Roman altar.

A fine ancient corridor of yews leads up to the church.

Henshaw, All Hallows

All Hallows was built in 1888-9 in Early English style. St Hilda features in a fine east window with glass by Ruth and Holman Hunt. A meeting room was added in 2000 and an electronic Copeman Hart, three-manual organ was installed in 2002.

Hexham Abbey, St Andrew

There has been a church on this site for over 1300 years since Queen Etheldreda made a grant of lands to Wilfrid, Bishop of York in about 674. Of Wilfrid's Benedictine abbey, the Saxon crypt and traces of an apsidal chapel still remain. In Norman times Wilfrid's abbey was replaced by an Augustinian priory. The church today is mainly that building of about 1170-1250, in Early English style. The choir, north and south transepts and the cloisters, where canons studied and meditated, date from this period. The nave appears to have been rebuilt in the fifteenth century. Since the Dissolution of the Monasteries in 1537 the abbey has been the parish church of Hexham.

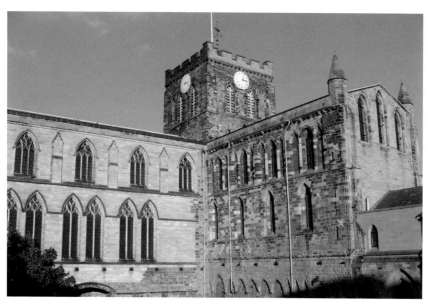

The east end was rebuilt in 1858-60 and the nave, whose walls incorporate some of the earlier church (including many decorated Roman and Anglo-Saxon stones), was built in 1907-9 by Temple Moore. In 1996 an additional chapel was created at the east end of the north choir aisle. Named St Wilfrid's Chapel, it offers a place for prayer or quiet reflection.

The superb early Saxon crypt itself reuses Roman stone, including two important inscriptions. An even more impressive Roman monument now stands at the foot of the Night Stairs in the south transept – a massive carved tombstone to Flavinius the Standard Bearer of the *Ala Petriana*, a 500-strong auxiliary unit stationed at Corbridge during the late first century and which had been raised in Gaul. Opposite this stands the partially reconstructed eighth-century cross, associated with Bishop Acca who died in 740.

The Frith Stool in the middle of the choir is a very fine, possibly seventh-century seat carved from a single block of sandstone.

The very fine wooden painted screen between the nave and choir was carved in the early sixteenth century. It may once have also been surmounted by a rood, but now supports the superb organ built in 1974 by Lawrence Phelps and Associates.

The glass is mostly nineteenth century, and includes work by C.E. Kempe, Henry Holliday and William Wailes.

Kirkhaugh, Holy Paraclete

Kirkhaugh is thought to be the only English church to be dedicated to the Holy Paraclete. The boundaries of the parish were described by the king of Scotland's justices at their Assizes at Nunwick in North Tynedale in 1258. The list of Rectors goes back to before 1432. The present building was consecrated in 1869 and designed by the then Rector, Octavius James. The steeply pitched hammerbeam roof and flèche spire are thought to have been inspired by the churches of the Black Forest.

The font comprises one octagonal bowl set on another bowl inverted with a short column between and was restored in 1889. The chalice, which is used regularly, was made in London in 1571. The wooden reredos was carved by Mildred James, one of the rector's daughters.

There is a Saxon 'hammerhead' cross in the churchyard set in a nineteenth-century base.

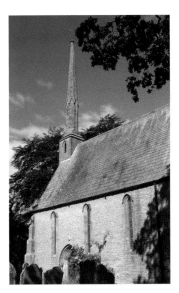

Knarsdale, St Jude

The first mention of a priest at Knarsdale dates from 1135. The present church was built in 1833 and entirely replaced an earlier building, which had become ruinous by 1810. It was then enlarged in 1892 and again in 1906 when the porch and vestry were added. The church seems to have had no dedication until it was put under the patronage of St Jude in 1968. The east window is by Kempe.

One of the memorials in the churchyard tells the sad tale of an intriguing murder mystery.

Lambley, St Mary and St Patrick

A small convent of Benedictine nuns once existed at Lambley. It was destroyed by the Scots in 1296, rebuilt and survived until the Dissolution of the Monasteries by Henry VIII. The church of St Mary and St Patrick was built in 1885 to a design by William Searle Hicks, in thirteenth-century style. It is a simple sandstone building without aisles.

Nenthead, St John

The church of St John the Evangelist was built and consecrated on land given by the London Lead Company in 1845. It was designed by local distinguished architects, Ignatius Bonomi and John A. Cory. It was financed by public subscription and built by local labour. It is (geographically speaking!) the highest church in England.

Newbrough, St Peter

A chapel was first recorded at Stanecroft (now Newbrough) around 1170, but there may have been a church here as early as the ninth century. The present St Peter's was opened in 1866 and extended between 1880 and 1883. It replaced a series of older buildings, with major rebuildings having taken place in 1292, 1732 and 1795. The lych-gate was added after the First World War.

The church was built beside a major Roman road – the Stanegate. In 1929 traces of Roman structures were found adjacent to the north wall of the church, perhaps a fortlet originally built in the first century. Evidence of fourth-century occupation was also found, along with signs of possible post-Roman activities.

A grave cover, possibly late thirteenth century, bearing the crude image of a sword can be seen in the porch.

Ninebanks, St Mark

St Mark's was first built in 1764 as a chapel of ease in the parish of Allendale. It was rebuilt in 1813 and then again in Early English style. The architect was F. Hasewell of North Shields. It is a small, neat stone structure, with a nave and a square tower topped by a stone spire.

St John Lee, St John of Beverley

There was possibly an oratory here in the seventh century, but the name of no incumbent is known until 1311. The medieval church was largely rebuilt in 1650 and again in 1818 (by John Dobson) and further modified in 1886 by W.S. Hicks when the building was widened and the spire added. The organ, by Nicholson, was probably also introduced at this time. It is a stone building with a plain tile roof, supported in the nave by fine carved timbers. A calvary designed by Leonard Evetts was added to the 1886 chancel screen in 1983.

A number of pieces of carved medieval stonework can be seen in the church, including the thirteenth-century effigy of a bishop. There are also three fine nineteenth-century hatchments and an unusual memorial in the form of a carved figure by Thomas Clapperton to Simon Mewburn, who was killed in action in the First World War.

In the baptistry there is a large stone, 'the Oakwood stone', with prehistoric 'cup and ring' carvings (such stones possibly had a religious or territorial function and were carved over a very long period, but many seem to date roughly to the years between 2000 and 1600BC).

A Roman altar also stands in the baptistry. The inscriptions were effaced and it was converted into a font and then (in the seventeenth century?) into a sundial when it was placed in the churchyard.

Warden, St Michael and All Angels

The first church at Warden is said to have been built by Saint Wilfrid in 704. The greater part of the present church, however, was built in 1764 by Sir Walter Blackett and was further altered in 1867 – especially the chancel. The oldest surviving feature in the body of the church is the eleventh-century (Saxon) arch connecting the nave with the base of the tower – the arch reuses many Roman stones. The tower has four successive stages, the bottom of which is probably the oldest Saxon tower in Northumberland. The windows depicting the four evangelists and the painted reredos are memorials to the Cruddas family (George Cruddas was incumbent from 1867 – 95).

Several medieval stone coffins and grave-covers are in the porch; these include the 'Warden Man', possibly a reused Roman altar, adapted in about 1100. There is also a well-preserved Saxon grave cover in the chancel. The fine lych-gate was built in 1903.

Whitfield, Holy Trinity

Holy Trinity replaced St John's as parish church in 1859-60, a gift of the then incumbent J.A. Blackett-Ord and his wife. It is a fine example of mid-Victorian Early English work by A.B. Higham, and, as the *1982 guide* says, it 'abounds in craftsmanship in stone, wood, wrought iron and glass … a beautiful church in a glorious setting: well worth a visit'. Pevsner describes it as 'ambitious'!

Whitfield, St John

There was a rector here in 1180, but the present, simple (and since 1859 truncated) stone building was built in 1790 by Newton.

Whitley Chapel, St Helen

A simple stone church of uncertain date, St Helen's is said to have been built in 1742 and to have been consecrated in 1764 by the Archbishop of York. Before this there was certainly a chapel of ease here in the parish of Hexham. Four wooden panels dated 1858 hang in the nave, inscribed with the Ten Commandments, Apostles' Creed and Lord's Prayer.

NEWCASTLE CENTRAL DEANERY

Brunswick Village, St Cuthbert

St Cuthbert's was built as a chapel of ease in 1905 in the parish of Dinnington. Its walls are of colliery bricks and decorative red facing bricks.

Brunton Park, St Aidan

The present (brick) church was consecrated in 1963 and replaced a Nissen hut that had been used since 1946. St Aidan's was designed by Fred Herron as a multi-purpose building, but has been adapted gradually for liturgical use.

Dinnington, St Matthew

The parish was created in 1818, but there are no baptism, marriage or burial records before 1835. The present church was dedicated in 1886 and was built at a cost of £3000 by Captain Henry Bell of Woolsington. The painted reredos, given to the church in 1959, was originally presented to the first Bishop of Newcastle in 1882 by the women of the diocese for his chapel at Benwell Towers. It was restored in 2005.

Fawdon, St Mary the Virgin

A daughter church of All Saints Gosforth, St Mary's is a simple, functional building consecrated in 1959. It was altered and extended in 1979 to become a dual-purpose church and hall.

Gosforth, All Saints

All Saints is an imposing Gothic revival church, built in 1855-7 by R.J. Johnson. The tower was added in 1896. It contains good woodwork by Ralph Hedley and a reredos by Johnson. The 1906 font is by Crawford and Hick. Glass is by Bayne, Bryans (in memory of the prolific church architect and builder W.S. Hicks in 1904) and Heaton, Butler and Bayne. There is a peal of 10 bells and an organ by Harrison and Harrison, which was rebuilt in 1929 and restored in 1994.

Gosforth, St Hugh

Another daughter church of All Saints Gosforth, St Hugh's is a simple brick building built in 1960 and extended in 1981.

Gosforth, St Nicholas

St Nicholas is the ancient parish church of Gosforth and may have been founded around 800. The medieval church thought to have been built in or by 1153 was replaced in 1798-9. Of this building, by John Dodds, the tower and west end survive, but it was substantially enlarged in 1818-20 by John Dobson, in the same elegant Georgian style. The south porch was built in 1833 and R.J. Johnson added a north porch when he restored the church in 1884. It was again extended in 1913 by Hicks and Charlewood and further work was carried out in 1959 when a clergy vestry was built. A fine new two-manual organ by Nicholson was installed in 1999.

There is a great deal of fine glass by Wailes, Kempe, Swaine, Bourne & Son and Evetts.

The registers show that in 1805 Edward Barrett married Mary Graham Clarke here – the parents of Elizabeth Barrett Browning.

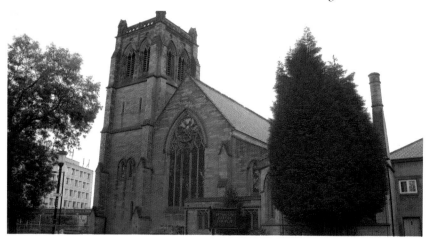

Jesmond, Clayton Memorial Church (Jesmond Parish Church)

The building (1857-61) was the last church to be designed by John Dobson and was one of the last Anglican churches built to contain galleries. It was designed so that there would be no particular distinction between the chancel and the nave and originally had a central pulpit. The intention was to express the evangelical convictions of the founders (previously members of St Thomas's Chapel where Richard Clayton was chaplain and Master of St Mary Magdalene Hospital). The design originally included a spire, but this was not built.

The vestry hall (1874) was designed by Austen and Johnson, the choir pews (1901), vestry (1903) and baptistry are the work of Hicks and Charlewood. The stained glass is by George Baguley, Atkinson Brothers of Newcastle and Lawrence Lee. The organ was originally (1863) in the west gallery, but was rebuilt in the north aisle in 1894. It was replaced in 1913 by the present instrument made by Rushworth and Dreaper.

Jesmond, Holy Trinity

Holy Trinity (War Memorial) Parish Church was built in 1920-2 by Hoare and Wheeler, although the chancel by Hicks and Charlewood dates from 1908. The high quality of craftsmanship and design is remarked on by Pevsner. The style is Decorated Gothic. The building is in the Decorated style, with windows by Nicholson Studios and a fine Rushworth and Dreaper organ. A reversible platform/dais and more functional communion rail were added in 1999.

Kenton, The Church of the Ascension

The Church of the Ascension was begun in 1954 on the site of the old Kenton Quarry. It was a daughter church of All Saints Gosforth and paid for by public subscription. The architects were Newcombe and Newcombe and the builders were J. and W. Lowry.

The roof is a unique single structure of pre-stressed concrete, supported on pillars. The walls were added later. In 1980 the rear nave was partitioned to form a hall and in 2001 the lower hall was refurbished to make a chapel. The chamber organ by Rushworth and Dreaper was installed in 1966.

Kingston Park, St John

St John's was the only church to be built in the diocese in the last decade of the twentieth century and is the focus of a local ecumenical project. The building incorporates a flexible worship space with a range of other rooms and facilities.

Newcastle, Cathedral Church of St Nicholas

For many years St Nicholas was a parish church, the fourth largest in England. The first church on the site was built soon after 1080. It was replaced around 100 years later and repaired and extended after twice being damaged by fire in the following century. In the later fourteenth century the walls were heightened to allow a clerestory to lighten the building. The simplicity of the form and architecture still marks the body of the church. The superb stone tower with its magnificent lantern was added by the end of the fifteenth century.

During the nineteenth century important work was carried out to stabilise the tower and the north side of the building and most of the stained glass we see now was fitted into the windows. Only one small but very beautiful fragment of medieval glass remains. It depicts Mary feeding the Christ child and can be found in the centre of the otherwise plain east window of St Margaret's Chapel. The glass in the windows of St George's chapel is in memory of local industrialists and a prominent politician, Viscount Grey, a founder of the Royal Society for the Protection of Birds, whose window is full of many kinds of birds and wildlife. The most recent glass was designed in 2002 by Mike Davis for the Danish Memorial Window in the north choir aisle. The monument below it, designed in 1982 by Ronald G. Sims, honours the 4,000 Danish merchant seamen who sailed from the Tyne during the Second World War and the 1406 who lost their lives.

An attempt had been made to create a bishopric at Newcastle in 1553 and to make St Nicholas a cathedral, but it was not until 1882 that the new diocese was formed. This brought major alterations to the interior of St Nicholas in the form of wood and stone fittings. The work was supervised by Robert J. Johnson and carried out by a number of craftsmen including Ralph Hedley (the rood screen and stalls), Robert Beall (the pulpit – to Johnson's design) and J.S. Westmacott (the reredos) – all to a very high standard. Johnson was commissioned by Wilberforce, the first Bishop of Newcastle, to design his furnishings in line with the English cathedral tradition and in late fifteenth-century Gothic style. For the decoration of the splendid canons' stalls and choir stalls, Ralph Hedley copied details from Exeter and Carlisle Cathedrals dating from 1401 to 1419.

The font and its beautiful carved canopy date from the early fifteenth century. Nearby is a carved marble monument of Admiral Lord Collingwood, the hero of the battle of Trafalgar in 1805. It was erected in 1821 and moved to its present position in 1931.

There is evidence of an organ at St Nicholas as early as 1503, but a fine new instrument was built by Renatus Harris in 1676. This was rebuilt and moved to the north transept between 1881 and 1891, the original case, for the most part, being used. It was twice later repaired and modified before being rebuilt in 1982 by Nicholson and Co.

Many monuments were cleared from St Nicholas in 1783. Amongst those that remain is the early seventeenth-century memorial to the Hall family on the west wall of St George's Chapel and the far grander Maddison Monument, of a similar date, on the west wall of the south transept. The most important earlier monument is a Flemish brass, said to be the largest brass altar cover in the country. It commemorates Roger Thornton, his wife and their seven children. It was made a little before 1492 and was moved to the cathedral from the ancient parish church of All Saints.

The vestries on the south side of the choir were built in 1736. A hall, library, further vestries and other rooms were added to the north-east side of the cathedral in 1926 and were extended in 1984.

Throughout the building there are images of St Nicholas, the patron saint of mariners and children, to be found.

The splendid cathedral clock was installed in 1761 and was extensively rebuilt in 1895. Since 1914 (and in addition to the large clock bell, provided in 1833 and recast in 1891) there has been a peal of 12 bells in the cathedral tower, plus three pre-Reformation bells, one of which is tolled to announce daily services.

Newcastle, St Andrew, Newgate Street

There is evidence of a Saxon church on the site of the present nave of St Andrew's, but this, possibly the oldest church in the city, is largely of twelfth-century form, though with many later alterations. The twelfth-century Romanesque chancel arch with its chevron ornamentation is very fine. The last addition to the building was the south porch, in baroque style, built in 1726, by which time the aisles had been widened, the chancel lengthened and the two transepts and the Trinity Chapel added. The building was damaged during the English Civil War when it came under fire after a gun was mounted on the top of the west tower. The south transept was remodelled in 1844 by John Dobson and a more thorough-going restoration by T. Oliver followed in 1866; still further work was carried out in the 1950s and 60s by Caroë and Robinson.

The medieval font cover, similar to that in St Nicholas Cathedral, is particularly fine. Other things to see include a leper's squint, the painting of the Last Supper by Giordano, which hangs in the baptistry, and the choir stalls, built in 1907 from Austrian oak. The pulpit and choir stalls are by Ralph Hedley. The royal arms of George IV are carved over the west door.

The organ (in the north chancel aisle) was built by Binns in 1895, rebuilt by Harrison and Harrison in 1971 and overhauled in 1999. Glasswork is by Kempe, Gibson and Evetts. There are six bells in the tower. They were cast by Richard Phelps of Whitechapel, London in 1726, and then recast and hung for stationary ringing in 1966.

A length of the medieval town wall can be seen in the churchyard.

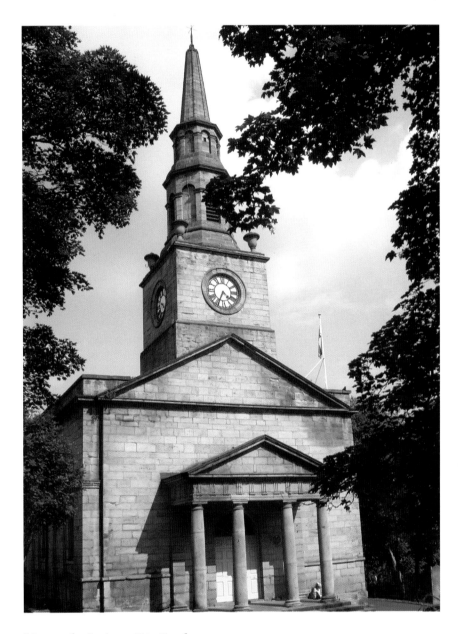

Newcastle, St Ann, City Road

St Ann's is a very elegant stone church built in 1764-8 in the English Renaissance style to a design by William Newton, a renowned local architect. It replaced a medieval building built in 1344. After the Reformation it seems that the chapel was neglected and during the reign of Elizabeth I was used as an emergency plague hospital. The stone for the present St Ann's is said to have been taken from the town wall. The reredos by Hicks and Charlewood was made in 1911. The building was carefully refurbished in 1998.

The churchyard was among the last within the city to be closed for burials and is the resting place of many who died in the last great cholera epidemic.

Newcastle, St Barnabas and St Jude

The current building is a conversion of the original 1907 hall. (The church building of St Barnabas next door was demolished and sheltered accommodation was built on site. St Jude's Church building is in Shieldfield, and was deconsecrated long ago.) The present Church Centre comprises a small chapel, good-sized hall, and two further rooms, plus kitchen, toilet facilities and store cupboard.

Newcastle, Christ Church, Shieldfield

Christ Church was built in 1859-61 by A.B. Higham, and is Victorian Gothic Decorated style with an elegant tower and broach spire.

Newcastle (Jesmond), St George

St George's was built in 1888-9 by Charles Mitchell, a local shipbuilder, who engaged his shipyard architect, Thomas Spence, to design the building.

St George's is an outstanding example of Victorian art and architecture. The exterior is perhaps deceptively simple, though the Italianate detached campanile in imitation of St Mark's, Venice dominates the local skyline. The restrained magnificence of the interior rewards careful exploration – the glass, mosaics, carving and metalwork display a masterful blend of a traditional Early English architecture with Art Nouveau.

The mosaics in the sanctuary are influenced by Ravenna. High on the walls of the sanctuary, to either side of the high altar, are twelve mosaic figures depicting the 12 apostles, each bearing an implement representing some part of their life or the manner of their death. The entire floor of the church is also laid with mosaic with rich patterns and symbols.

The altar and reredos are of white pavanozza marble, by Emley and Sons of Newcastle, as are the two top steps of the sanctuary steps; the third step is of rouge jasper and the fourth and fifth of Sienna marble. The altar table is a solid block of marble 10ft long and carved with great skill. The stained glass was made by Gateshead Stained Glass Co., except for the two west aisle windows by O'Neil Brothers. The woodcarving is by Ralph Hedley.

The four-manual organ was built by Lewis and Co. of London, in 1887. It was reconstructed in 1904 by Binns and in 1993 was overhauled and partially rebuilt by Harrison and Harrison of Durham. There is a peal of eight bells.

Newcastle (Jesmond), St Hilda

St Hilda's was built in 1905 by Hicks and Charlewood as the daughter church of St George's. It features a hanging pyx in the Lady Chapel, the only one in the diocese. The war memorial triptych, painted by F.H. Newbury, depicts the Virgin, Jesus, St Hilda and St Nicholas along with a Cullercoats fishwife, a miner, an engineer, a shipman, a sailor, a soldier, a Roman centurion and an Norman king/knight.

Newcastle, St John the Baptist, Grainger Street

Although St John's was probably first built in the twelfth century, the greater part of the church dates from the fourteenth and fifteenth centuries, including the capless arcades and the timber roof structures. The north transept and south aisles were built in the mid-fourteenth century, as was the north aisle, which was later widened and lengthened. The western aisle was added to the north transept in the late fourteenth century. A clerestory was added in the second half of the fifteenth century along with a new roof; the south aisle was widened and lengthened and the south transept and tower vault were built by Robert Rhodes.

A blocked fourteenth-century window high on the outer north wall of the sacristy and a cross-shaped aperture in the north wall of the chancel support documentary evidence that the sacristy was once the lodgings for an anchorite.

In the late eighteenth century the north-west corner of the north aisle was pared to allow a new road to be built – what was to become Grainger Street. The south and east walls of the chancel were rebuilt in 1848 by John Dobson.

The linen-fold panelling was added to the sanctuary in 1875. The high altar, organ case (1909) and room beam (1926) are all the work of Sir Charles Nicholson. The choir stalls are by Robert Thompson of Kilburn. The fine wrought iron chancel screen and communion rails are the work of Stephen Dykes-Bower and were installed when the church was reordered in 1965-73.

The font was given to the church in 1689. The canopy dates from the early sixteenth century and was restored in the seventeenth century. The pulpit is late seventeenth-century and was restored in 1969-71.

The stained glass includes a few glass fragments of medieval glass, now in the north chancel window, among them the earliest known representation of the city (then town) arms.

Amongst the monuments is a memorial (1888) on the wall of the south aisle to the great builder and architect Richard Grainger (1797-1861).

The organ was built by Harrison and Harrison in 1909 and rebuilt in 1996. There is a peal of eight bells, recast by Gillett and Johnston in 1926.

Newcastle, St Luke, Spital Tongues

A brick church built in 1892 to a design by Newcastle architect H. W. Wood to replace a corrugated iron mission church.

Newcastle, St Thomas the Martyr, Barras Bridge

St Thomas's was built between 1827 and 1830 by the famous Newcastle architect John Dobson, on the site of an old leper hospital. It is Dobson's first church but perhaps also his finest. It replaced a medieval chapel that stood at the north end of the Swing Bridge. It is in Gothic style and is loosely modelled on the chancel of the Temple Church in London. The gallery was added in 1837.

The stained glass was added in and after 1881, much of it the work of the studio of George Joseph Baguley of Newcastle. The very fine three-manual organ is by Harrison and Harrison and was commissioned in 1961.

St Thomas's is highly unusual in that it was built by the City under Act of Parliament and is neither a parish church nor a 'peculiar' but is governed by Acts of Parliament, with the Master and Wardens forming a Body Corporate.

There are four important war memorials in and around the church grounds commemorating those who died in the Boer, First and Second World Wars.

North Gosforth, St Columba

The first St Columba's was built in about 1865. The present building was erected in the 1980s to replace both this and St Chad's, Woodlands Park.

NEWCASTLE EAST DEANERY

Byker, St Anthony of Egypt

A stone church built by Lord Northbourne and dedicated in 1868.

Byker, St Martin

The first St Martin's was built in 1933 and demolished in June 2005. St Martin's Centre was built 2005-2006, opened in May 2006 and formally dedicated on 15 July 2006. The building includes a chapel and a highly flexible 'hall' space with partitions, with two meeting spaces for both formal and informal activities, and full industrial standard catering facilities plus a community kitchen.

Two small windows by Evetts installed in the 1970s in memory of the Mutch family are being refurbished for installation as free-standing pieces in St Martin's Centre. The chapel of St Martin's Centre contains a substantial piece of stained-glass art by the local artist Cate Watkinson. Based on motifs of overlapping circles it celebrates the new beginning for the local community that St Martin's Centre represents, but a beginning that has continuity with a rich local history. There are other pieces of glass by Cate Watkinson throughout the building. A Makin electronic organ will be installed early in 2007.

Byker, St Michael
and All Angels with St Lawrence

St Michael's Church was built in 1862-3, in Decorated style to a design by the Edinburgh architect W.L. Moffat. The north aisle was added in 1936. It occupies a distinctive site in the heart of the Byker Estate overlooking the Tyne Gorge. Much of the church wall, which dates back to the nineteenth century, is still in place as a boundary for the site. In the 1970s the church became isolated by the Byker redevelopment. From 2001 the PCC has been seeking to redevelop the church site in line with the wishes of the local community, including the themes of arts, heritage and culture. The Conversation Plan for the Byker Estate (published 2004) indicates the overall significance of the parish church.

St Michael's Church, its boundary wall and ground were a dramatic piece of townscape before the redevelopment, built high on a precipice overlooking Byker's amphitheatre. It represents the peak notionally and literally of continuity from old to new and is the only place in the Estate where passers-by can be completely cocooned in old Byker. Its spire (and with the recent demolition of the hall, the main west façade) can be seen across the Estate and well beyond to the south and west for many miles, and represents Byker's most visible and enduring landmark.

Byker, St Silas

St Silas was designed by R.J. Johnson and consecrated in 1886 and altered in 1899. It has recently been completely reordered as part of an award-winning £2 million redevelopment project to form a community hall, which includes a worship space and is linked to a 20-unit housing scheme, which provides accommodation for single homeless adults.

Longbenton, St Bartholomew

There has been a church at Longbenton since at least the twelfth century (the first known priest was in 1150), but it is quite possible that the first church here was very much earlier. The church was rebuilt (and the dedication changed from St Andrew to St Bartholomew) in 1790-1. Subsidence necessitated that the chancel was rebuilt in 1855 and then in 1873-5 the south aisle and organ chamber were added by R.J. Johnson. In 1888 the choir and clergy vestry was built on the north side of the chancel by W.S. Hicks and in 1891 a peal of eight bells was installed. The main remnant of the late eighteenth-century building is the tower with its short spire. There have been numerous additions and alterations since, including the construction of an octagonal church hall in 1980 and St Andrew's Chapel in 1994.

There are windows by Leonard Evetts including plain glass in the chancel, the Addison window in the south transept (1993) and a set of 10 memorial windows in the chapel/vestry extension (1994). Evetts also painted the icon, dedicated in 1980, which depicts the annunciation, on the wall behind the lectern. The font dates from 1857. The elaborate oak reredos was installed in 1902.

There are a number of monuments in the church including two medieval grave-slabs and several sixteenth- to eighteenth-century ledger stones (which were previously set into the chancel floor). The organ was built by Binns, Fitton and Haley Ltd of Bramley, Leeds in 1932.

Balliol College has been patron of St Bartholomew's since 1340.

Longbenton, St Mary Magdalene

A daughter church of St Bartholomew's Longbenton, St Mary's is a simple brick building completed in 1957. The font, which once served as a sundial support in St Bartholomew's churchyard, probably dates to around 1200.

Newcastle (High Heaton), St Francis

The original mission church of St Francis, a wooden building, held its first service in August 1935. It was blessed by Bishop Bilbrough on 4 October 1935. The present church was completed in 1953 and designed by the architectural practice of N.B. Edwards and built by Stanley Miller Ltd. The building is a particularly good example of post-war architecture. The austerity of its design reflects a time of stress, shortages and hope for the future. The church was built to strict cash limits and under a system of building licences. The side chapel (dedicated to the Holy Cross) was added in 1957.

There is a memorial window of St Francis by Evetts (1957), who is also responsible for a painted cross above the side chapel altar, influenced by the San Damiano Cross of Francis.

A new oak and glass screen was commissioned and built at the back of the chapel for the fiftieth anniversary celebrations, also with a Franciscan theme.

Newcastle (Heaton), St Gabriel

The foundation stone of St Gabriel's was laid in 1898. The church was designed by Frank Rich and built, in stages, by Walter Baston. The nave and south transept were consecrated in 1899. The chancel, tower, organ chamber, north aisle and north transept followed in 1905. New vestries were dedicated in 1910. Finally, the Lady Chapel,

south transept, screens, a new window, lectern, font, chancel screen and reredos were completed in 1931 by H.L. Hicks.

The font is polished granite, with a carved canopy in memory of Canon Trotter, Vicar from 1902-32. The nave is dominated by the impressive rood carved by the Ralph Hedley workshop, who also carved the lectern, pulpit, screens and altar rails. A large carved and coloured triptych topped by the figure of Christ in majesty is prominent behind the altar – above which is the large mural of the ascension by J. Eadie Reid, who also did three smaller paintings on the altar.

The north aisle accommodates the organ, built by Abbott and Smith in 1906 and overhauled and repaired in 2005.

The Lady Chapel contains a copy of the Bishop's Bible of 1568, known as the 'Treacle Bible'.

Walker, Christ Church

Christ Church was built in 1848 to a design by A.B. Higham in late thirteenth-century style. The chancel was later lengthened and the larger five-light west window was added along with the tower and spire and the south aisle. Some very fine stained glass can be seen especially in the west window, which is by Kempe. It depicts Christ in glory surrounded by northern saints.

The pews were removed in the 1980s and a nave altar has been installed on a platform. Apart from the chancel, the whole church is now carpeted, with loose chairs, and a low-ceilinged entrance lobby/meeting room has been built across the west end. The octagonal hall to the north was built in 1988 and is connected to the church through lobbies and a kitchen, with office and toilets.

The churchyard is very extensive, at one time reputedly the largest in England. It includes a fine memorial to Robert Chambers, nineteenth-century 'aquatic champion of England', a great oarsman.

Walkergate, St Oswald

St Oswald's was built in 1932 in the form of two brick-built halls, the lower of which serves as a worship space.

NEWCASTLE WEST DEANERY

Benwell, St James

St James was designed by John Dobson in 1831-2, according to Pevsner his first use of Norman style. It includes an unusual 'queen-post' ceiling. It was built by Richard Grainger, whose grave is in the churchyard along with those of many other notable figures from nineteenth-century Newcastle life. Dobson was also responsible for an extension to the building in 1864 when the nave and south aisle were built (the latter has served as the church hall since 1974). Vestries were added in 1879-80, the spire, choir vestry and porch in 1895 (by Hicks and Charlewood) and the north aisle in 1902. There is a ring of six bells by Charles Carr of Smethwick and some fine glass. The organ was moved from the redundant church of St Cuthbert, Melbourne Street in 1974.

Benwell, St John

A simple dual-purpose building built in 1949-50.

Benwell, Venerable Bede

This church is notable in that it was completed in 1937 to a design by Professor W.B. Edwards in 1930s Art Deco style. It is built in brick and pantiles and replaced an early twentieth-century wooden church.

Chapel House, Holy Nativity

A brick building completed in 1972 to a design by John Kirkham. The M-shaped roof gives an internal impression of height and was designed to look 'like arms raised in prayer' but is more often thought to be like angel's wings or a crib. Interior artwork by Charles Samesbury of Allendale includes a sculpted metal cross on the east wall behind the altar and a stylised 'Star of Bethlehem' in the entrance foyer.

Cowgate, St Peter

St Peter's was built in 1952. A simple brick structure it includes above the altar a Christus Rex carved from wood from Holy Island by Kathleen Parbury and on the walls a set of plaster Stations of the Cross.

Denton, Holy Spirit

A red-brick church to a design by Newcombe and Newcombe, it was partly modelled on the chapel of the Society of the Sacred Mission at Kelham and was completed in 1956, with a narthex added in 1966 and a hall in 1980.

Fenham, St James and St Basil

The church was begun in 1927 and completed in 1931. Sir James Knott paid for the church, vicarage and parish hall in memory of his sons, James and Basil, who were killed in the 1914-18 war. Designed by Eric Edward Lofting, assistant surveyor to the fabric of Westminster Abbey, it has been hailed by some (but Pevsner is not among them) as a masterpiece and one of the last great churches of the Arts and Crafts Movement in England. Alexander Pringle Ltd of Gateshead was the main contractor.

It was built on a reinforced concrete raft to protect the building from old mine-workings. It is faced in beautifully tooled sandstone from nearby Kenton Quarry. The main body of the

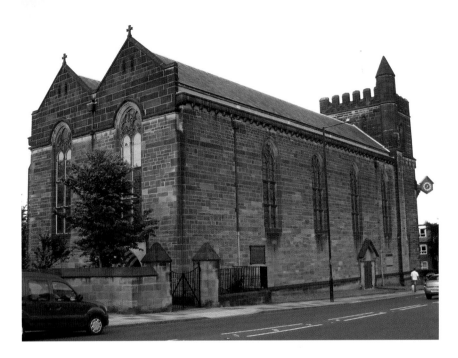

church has a single arcade of four and a half bays running down the spine of the building, dividing the space into two immensely tall (45.5ft) and virtually identical aisles. The tower is 65ft high with an additional 9ft for the cupola. Carved wood by Lawrence Turner and stained glass by Woore and Jack are special features of an otherwise plain (almost austere) interior. The Ten Commandments are carved on the north wall of the sanctuary. The font was made by J.G. Cook from Heptonwood stone from Yorkshire. The foundation stone is said to be Roman in origin.

Two emblems seen in the church have special meanings – the cockle-shell, the emblem of St James the Great, and the dove, the emblem of St Basil the Great of Caesarea, who wrote treatise on the Holy Spirit.

The three-manual organ is by J.W. Walker and Sons Ltd. of London. There is a unique chime of 17 bells cast by Mears and Stainbank of Whitechapel. Eight are rung full circle in the traditional English manner by rope and wheel; nine are hung 'dead', sounded by drawing the clapper across to strike the inner side of the bell. All 17 can be played like a carillon from a clavier in the ringing room. An inscription on the tenor bell reads: 'We ring in memory of James and Basil Knott. God knows'.

Low Elswick, St Stephen

Only the spire (built in 1868) remains from the Victorian St Stephen's. It houses a fine ring of eight bells. The simple adjacent chapel was opened in 1986.

Milbourne, Holy Saviour

This chapel of ease on the Milbourne Estate was begun in 1867, probably by R.J. Johnson. It remains an unspoilt example of Victorian Gothic, with chancel, nave, vestry and porch. It has a 'broach' spire. The fittings are all from 1869.

Newbiggin Hall, St Wilfrid

St Wilfrid's was completed in 1967. It is supposed to represent an upturned coble or fishing boat. It is in a diamond form with the corners of the building pointing to the points of the compass. In the early 1990s the building was adapted: the extent of the glazed areas was reduced, double glazing installed and the seating was modernised.

Newburn, St Michael and All Angels

St Michael's is said to have been built around 1070 to replace a wooden church burned down in 1067, but there are hints in the form of a pre-Conquest sculpture reused in the east end of the chancel and some of the stones of the nave that an earlier stone building existed here.

The church has a four-bay nave with transepts. The north aisle is said to date to about 1175 and the south aisle in Early English style to 1250. There is a 'weeping' chancel. The tower is said to have been begun in 1070 but it also echoes pre-Conquest building styles and probably makes use of stones from Hadrian's Wall. It was used by the Scottish army in 1640 as a gun platform during their defeat of the English at the Battle of Newburn. The north transept was turned into a war memorial in 1951.

Most of the internal fittings are from the late nineteenth century. Vestries and a porch were built by W.S. Hicks in 1885 and 1896. The 1885 chancel screen and pulpit are the work of Ralph Hedley; the choir stalls and oak panelling were added in 1898. The reredos was brought from a disused church in Italy and is in the form of a triptych with doors. It bears paintings of angels ministering to Christ.

A ring of six bells was hung in 1888, the earliest of which is sixteenth century. The organ is by Nicholson (1885) and the glass is nineteenth century. That in the east end of the chancel was made in the nearby Lemington glass works.

A major fire in the tower in March 2006 seriously damaged the church. A full restoration is planned. The fine lych-gate, built by W.S. Hicks in 1896, was restored in 2005.

St Michael's has associations with George Stephenson (who was married here in 1802), and the Delaval and Hedley families (William Hedley the railway pioneer is buried in the churchyard).

Newcastle, Holy Cross (Fenham)

Holy Cross was built in 1935-6 by H.L. Hicks on land given by John Blackett-Ord using nineteenth-century bricks reused from Heaton Hall. There is a fine small organ in the west gallery by Nigel Church and Company of Stamfordham and a circular window by Evetts. The slender tower at the north-west corner, surmounted by a gilded cross is a conspicuous landmark in the west of the city.

Newcastle, St Matthew with St Mary

St Matthew's was built in 1877 to a design by R.J. Johnson and is considered by some to be his finest work. The 1896 reredos is a memorial to him raised by his colleagues and family. The tower was built by Hicks and Charlewood in 1895.

The tower houses a ring of eight bells; the two-manual organ by Nigel Church and Company was acquired and modified in 1980. There is some fine glass by Kempe and others.

Ponteland, St Mary

Tenth-century sculpture suggests that there was a church on this site by the late Saxon period but the earliest parts of the standing structure date to the twelfth century. This is the date of the lower part of the tower, with its fine west door, as well as the responds at the west end of the north arcade and the west side of the south transept. Excavations in 1983 suggested that this church originally had an apsidal east end.

Much of the present structure dates to the thirteenth century: this is the date of the long chancel and north transept, both of which preserve windows of that date. Fourteenth-century work is represented by the main east window and other windows in the chancel as well as the south arcade and south aisle windows. There is fifteenth-century work in the south transept. A series of restoration works in the Victorian period (1861 and 1880 by Wilson) was responsible for the current roofing and for the raised chancel floor. In the 1970s a central altar was introduced and the chancel cleared for congregational seating whilst choir and clergy vestries were placed in the tower; a kitchen and toilet block were also added.

Rare fragments of medieval (fourteenth-century) glass survive in the chancel and there are fine memorials to the Ogle family. A ring of six bells was installed in 2001. The organ was built by E.J. Johnson and Son, Cambridge in 1973.

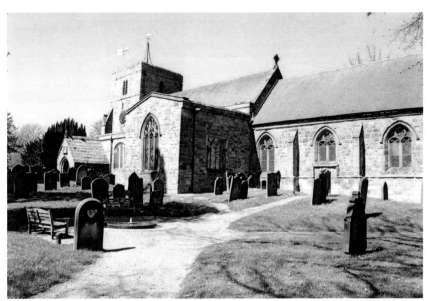

Scotswood, St Margaret of Antioch

Built in 1916-7 in stone, St Margaret's was converted to a 'Church and Parish Centre' in 2000. The west third of the building remains as a place of worship. The ground floor also comprises a hall with children's toilets off, an entrance lobby, with kitchen and toilets, and two small rooms (one used as a chapel). The first floor has a hall, two small offices and toilets. The second floor has a meeting room, a 'robing room' and gallery (where the organ is located, a single manual instrument, formerly in Cambois Parish Church) over the place of worship.

Sugley, Holy Saviour

Holy Saviour was designed by Benjamin Green of Newcastle who was also responsible for the Theatre Royal. Charles Bulmer laid the foundation stone on 24 June 1836. A William IV silver coin was placed in a glass vessel and sunk in the foundations. The church is built in Early English style and runs north to south instead of the usual east to west owing to the existence of a disused pit shaft on the east side. It was built as a chapel of ease to Newburn and became a separate parish fifty years later in 1887.

The east window is by William Wailes, probably from a design by Pugin. The present two-manual organ by Nelson and Co. of Durham was a gift from Bell's Close Chapel.

A plain life-size wooden cross was erected in about 1950 to the east of the church in the open space at the site of the mineshaft.

Throckley, St Mary

A simple stone church completed in 1887 by W.S. Hicks, according to Pevsner 'in the spirit of the late twelfth century'. There is good glasswork by Baguley and by Burlison and Grylls.

Whorlton, St John

St John's was built in 1866 as a chapel of ease of the parish of Newburn. It became a separate parish church in 1899. In 1911 there was an ambitious programme to rebuild it completely. The first phase of this was completed in 1911 by demolition of the east end of the church (where the rounded apse was) and its replacement with a new, much taller sanctuary.

The second phase of this plan was to knock down the rest of the original church and build a much larger church with three aisles. In preparation for that second phase, doorways were built and a much larger sanctuary arch was constructed. For some reason the work was never completed, possibly because of the First World War, and so St John's remains a unique mix of the original nave and new sanctuary.

A fine stained-glass window was dedicated in 1999 to celebrate the centenary of the parish. It was designed by Duncan Storr and made by Mark Smith. The organ (1906) is by Harrison and Harrison.

TYNEMOUTH DEANERY

Backworth, St John the Baptist

A small stone church built in 1886 by the Taylor family of Chipchase Castle.

Balkwell, St Peter

A simple brick building opened in 1938. The organ (1940) is by Harrison and Harrison.

Billy Mill, St Aidan

A simple brick building first opened in 1955, extended in 1958 and in 1976.

Cullercoats, St George

John Loughborough Pearson was commissioned by the sixth Duke of Northumberland to build a church in memory of his father in 1878. It was completed in local sandstone, and consecrated in 1884. Pearson's design is a unique interpretation of thirteenth-century French Gothic architecture. The massing is confident, emphasised by the striking tower with its soaring broach spire (together 180 feet high), and the completely stone-vaulted interior (the only example in Northumberland) has a grandeur which only Pearson could achieve. There is an obvious family resemblance to Pearson's contemporary cathedral at Truro.

Stained glass by Kempe and Tower in the apse and side aisles is complemented by Leonard Evetts's baptistry windows. The furnishings throughout are of oak. The 1885 two-manual T.C. Lewis organ is widely recognised as one of the finest instruments of the period. It is the only unaltered Lewis organ remaining in the diocese.

Earsdon, St Alban

The present St Alban's was built in 1836 to a design by John and Benjamin Green, partly on the eastern portion of the site of the former church which may date to the thirteenth century. Before 1259 the church was under the care of the monks of Tynemouth, who in their turn were ruled from the great Benedictine monastery at St Albans. This may explain how Earsdon's church became dedicated to the first British martyr.

The building is in stone, in Early English style, consisting of a chancel (added in 1889), a nave of six bays and an embattled western tower with pinnacles. In 1874 Lord Hastings of Delaval Hall presented two lancet windows of glass that he had obtained in 1840 from Hampton Court Palace. It is believed to have been made originally by the famous Galyon Hone in 1531 at the order of King Henry VIII. Traces of Tudor crests and arms can be clearly seen. In 1958 the lancet windows in the east of the nave were restored by Leonard Evetts.

A memorial stone to the Hartley Mine Disaster of 12 January 1862 is in the north-east side of the church. The bodies of many of the 204 men and boys who died that terrible day are buried in the churchyard under another monument – a tall, corniced pedestal supporting an obelisk.

Marden, St Hilda
St Hilda's was opened in 1966 and shows a French influence in its design. It is built in brick.

Monkseaton, St Mary the Virgin
A substantial brick building completed in 1931 and extended to include a baptistry and entrance vestibule in 1964.

Monkseaton, St Peter
Like St Mary's, another substantial brick building and also originally a daughter church of St Paul's, Whitley Bay. It was completed in 1938 and had to be repaired after bomb damage suffered shortly afterwards, during the Second World War. There are three windows by Leonard Evetts and the two-manual organ is by Blacket and Howden. St Peter's was reordered internally in 2002.

North Shields, Christ Church

Christ Church was built to replace the parish church of St Mary, which stood within the walls of Tynemouth Castle. A survey by Oliver Cromwell's Commissioners in 1652 reported that the parish church was ruined and that North Shields was a sufficiently populous place to have a parish church built there.

The original building, built by Robert Trollope, was cruciform and the spaces between the arms of the cross were built over as demand for seating grew. It was consecrated in 1668. The tower was added in 1786-8, followed by a major restoration of the whole building in 1792-3 by John Dodds. Further changes were made in 1869. In 1951 interior restoration was carried out to remove some of the less pleasant aspects of Georgian and Victorian architecture. The organ and Victorian choir stalls were removed to the west gallery and the Mariners' Chapel of St Nicholas made. The parish centre was added in 1984.

On either side of the chancel windows hang decalogue boards made in 1785 containing the Creed, Lord's Prayer and Ten Commandments. The ornate plaster ceiling of the chancel incorporates symbols depicting the Trinity.

The windows were damaged during the Second World War and were re-glazed in 1952. Leonard Evetts is responsible for a chancel window, which commemorates the centenary of the RNLI.

The organ was purchased in 1794 and is said to have come from Vauxhall Gardens in London. It is housed in a mahogany case with side panels taken from HMS Calliope, a corvette built in 1884. There is a ring of 10 bells. Six date from 1788 and the remaining four from 1847 and 1878.

Two model sailing ships on top of the oak screen separating the Mariners' Chapel and the Chancel are builders' models dating from about 1820.

The parish stocks on the wall beneath the gallery originally stood opposite the church and were used as late as 1832.

North Shields, St Augustin

On 18 November 1888 St Augustin's was the first church to be consecrated by Bishop Wilberforce in the new Diocese of Newcastle. The chancel was added in 1888 and the two-story vestries in 1954. In 1998-9 the interior was reordered to include a meeting room, kitchen and toilets.

The pulpit originally stood in St Nicholas Cathedral where Bishop Wilberforce preached from it on the occasion of his enthronement. There are fine windows by Martin Travers, Reed and Millican and others. The three- (originally two-) manual organ was built by Foster and Andrews in 1867 and moved to St Augustin's in 1885. It was restored in 2000.

Shiremoor, St Mark

The present St Mark's succeeds an earlier building opened in 1889. It was consecrated and opened for worship on 4 November 1967. Designed by Ian Curry, St Mark's is thought by those who worship there – and others – to be one of the few success stories of 1960's church architecture. Of modern polygonal design with a free-standing altar of Northumberland slate and congregational seating on three sides of the altar, the building lends itself to an intimate style of worship in which priest and people may freely and easily engage. The beautiful Lady Chapel (recently refurbished) is separated from the nave by a clear glass screen which allows the two worship areas to blend together seamlessly. Under the same roof and with direct access from the church is a versatile hall with a well-equipped kitchen.

Tynemouth, St John Percy

St John's was designed by Anthony Salvin for the Fourth Duke of Northumberland and opened in 1864. It is a simple stone building with nave, chancel and two aisles. A hall was added in 1977. In 1999 St John's was completely and imaginatively reordered internally for multi-purpose use. The organ is by Nelson of Durham and was a gift from Percy Main Methodist Church in 1979.

Tynemouth, St Paul Cullercoats

St Paul's is a stone church built in Early English Gothic style in 1863-4 by Salvin. It has a ring of eight bells. The lych-gate was built in 1894 by W.S. Hicks.

Tynemouth Priory, Holy Saviour

Holy Saviour was designed by John and Benjamin Green in Perpendicular style. The foundation stone was laid in 1839 and the building was completed and consecrated in 1841. It had a nave, chancel and short transepts, but no aisles. Between 1882 and 1884 the chancel was enlarged, an organ chamber was built (now a side chapel) and new vestries were added. The tower at the west end was surmounted by a 95ft-high spire, until it became unsafe and had to be removed in about 1949. The present organ was installed in 1952, with the pipe-work housed in the (now reduced) west gallery. The porch at the west door was built in 1972.

The panelled reredos and chancel fittings are by W.S. Hicks. The glass is mostly late nineteenth-century (by Cottier, T.S. Curtis (Ward and Hughes), Powell Bros, Payne and Wailes and Strang), but the vestibule window contains old German glass, possiby from the seventeenth century. Leonard Evetts was responsible for the window in the south transept installed in 1946, and the fine millennium window installed in 2004 in the porch is the work of Effie Burns. It is designed to be touched as well as to be seen. The fine parish centre with meeting rooms, toilets and office was opened in 2006.

Wallsend, St John the Evangelist

St John's was built in 1955-6. It is a red brick structure with interior fittings of American oak with hand-crafted pews and doors by apprentices from the Swan Hunter shipyard. A *Christus Rex* (in carved stone) hangs behind the high altar, the work of Charles Sansbury of Allendale. The two-manual tracker organ is by Harrison and Harrison.

Wallsend, St Luke

St Luke's, the 'Shipyard Church', was built in grey stone in Early English Gothic style in 1885-7 by Oliver and Leeson and was extended in 1906. The very fine east window was installed in 1922, the work of Wilhelmina Geddes of Dublin – a crucifixion scene dedicated to the memory of those parishioners who died in the First World War.

Wallsend, St Peter

St Peter's was built in 1807-9 to replace, on a new site, the medieval church of Holy Cross (the ruins of which can still be seen – a twelfth-century church with a seventeenth-century porch). In 1892 the church was 'gothicized' by W.S. Hicks: the interior was gutted, a new roof and windows installed and the spire removed.

The chief architectural glory of St Peter's is its collection of twentieth-century Irish glass, the largest in England, and, as at St Luke's, the work of Wilhelmina Geddes. The Harrison and Harrison organ was installed in 1996 when the interior of the church was again reordered.

The stocks on the west wall of the tower were made in 1816. The victims of two mining disasters are buried in the churchyard: Heaton in 1815, which claimed 75 men and boys, and Wallsend Colliery in 1835, in which 102 men and boys died.

Willington, Good Shepherd (Battle Hill)

The Church of the Good Shepherd was designed to serve a Local Ecumenical Partnership and was built in brick in 1983. It is multi-functional. The kitchen was enlarged in 2003.

Willington, St Mary the Virgin

St Mary's was built to a design by Austin and Johnson in 1876. The rood screen was added in 1900. The 'Care Centre' meeting room, kitchen and toilets were added in 1987.

The memorial stained-glass windows for members of the Burn family who died in 1871 and 1872 are of interest in that they incorporate into the design photographic images of those commemorated. The two-manual organ, built in 1891, is by Harrison and Harrison.

Willington Quay, St Paul

St Paul's was built in 1876 and is a fairly typical late nineteenth-century stone-built structure with slated roofs. Its chancel, organ chamber and vestries were added in 1923, in memory of those who lost their lives in the 1914-18 war.

The exterior of the building remains virtually as built. However, across the years the interior has undergone extensive changes. In the 1970s, the pews were replaced with chairs, the wooden chancel screen and the font were repositioned and the high altar replaced with a brick and concrete nave altar. It was completely refurbished externally and internally reordered in 2000 to provide space for community activities as well as worship. At that time, a kitchen, toilets, small meeting room and IT training facilities were integrated into the west of the building and in the former aisles. In addition, two new screens were installed at the back of the nave (fixed) and at the chancel crossing (folding). Externally, a small soft-play area was laid.

A war memorial to those killed in the 1939-45 war was installed in 1948 and is incorporated into the housing for a processional cross.

ALNWICK DEANERY

Acklington, St John the Divine

St John's is a fine Victorian Gothic building designed in 1860 by James Deacon. Its stones were tooled and dressed at Alnwick Castle. Some good modern woodwork includes the altar, reredos and communion rails.

The attractive lych-gate was renovated on the occasion of the Coronation of Queen Elizabeth II on 2 June 1953.

Alnham, St Michael and All Angels

A medieval church was built in about 1200, but it appears to lie on Saxon foundations. The 'Transitional' chancel arch was probably raised in the early thirteenth century around the time when the church was given to the monks of Alnwick Abbey by the lord of the manor, William de Vescy. The outside of the north wall of the nave shows traces of an arcade, evidence of a demolished north aisle. The building was restored in 1870 by F.R. Wilson. The sanctuary was refurbished in 1938 when the east window, altar, panelling, communion rails and priest's desk were given in memory of Adam Scott. Further restoration work was carried out in 1953. The font bears the date 1664 and the bell is inscribed 'Alnham Nov. 1759'.

There are four medieval tomb covers in the floor of the chancel. Rather delightfully, the two on the north side are marked 'his' and those on the south side 'hers'! More somberly, a gravestone set in the back of the church records a drowning in the River Tweed.

Alnmouth, St John the Baptist

St John's, the third parish church to be built in the village, was built in Victorian Early English style by public
subscription between 1874 and 1876 on land donated
by Algernon, the Sixth Duke of Northumberland. The
south transept was added in 1880. The sanctuary ceiling
is noteworthy both for its superb shape and also for the
quality of its decoration. The pulpit is fine too, carved
with statues of soldier saints and of the Passion. There is
some good Victorian glass and six windows by Leonard
Evetts illustrating saintly monks. A seventh window by
Evetts on the theme of creation is in the porch. The
three-manual organ is by Nicholson and Newbegin.

Alnwick, St Michael

There are few traces of the building which existed
before 1147 when Alnwick Abbey was founded. The
present church dates from the fourteenth century, but
has been restored several times, most notably in 1464,
which endowed it with some of the finest architecture in the Perpendicular style in the north. More
recently it was restored in 1863 when the fourth
Duke of Northumberland employed Anthony Salvin
to complete the work. One of the most interesting
features is the spacious chancel, which provided seats
for the twenty-two canons of the ancient Alnwick
Abbey.

Among the interesting fittings are two fourteenth-
century tombs with figures of a man in a tunic and
a lady, a third medieval figure which appears to be a
cleric and a handsome fourteenth-century Flemish
carved chest. There is a large collection of fine Victorian
glass by Atkinson, Baguley, Burlison and Grylls, Clayton
and Bell, Lavers Barraud and Westlake, Powell and Ward
and Hughes.

Alwinton, St Michael and All Angels

St Michael's may have Saxon beginnings (one small
window suggests this, as does one of the quoins at the
south-east corner of the building), but the first record
of the parish is from the thirteenth century. The nave
and chancel arch and small choir were probably built
by the eleventh century. The chancel was rebuilt and
lengthened in the twelfth century and narrow aisles
were added to the nave. The arcading for these is in
Transitional style. In the thirteenth century a south
chapel or aisle transept was added to the nave.

The most striking feature of the church is the height of the chancel floor – well above that of the nave. This is partly to accommodate the steep slope on which the church is built, but also because a crypt was made under the floor in the early fourteenth century for the Clennell family.

After major repairs in 1724, the building was heavily 'restored' in 1851-2 by the Durham architect George Pickering. Much of the nave was rebuilt along with the south porch. A vestry was added. All that remains of the medieval church are the foundations of the north aisle and of the chancel arch, the chancel steps and part of the chancel itself. The Victorian stained glass is all by Wailes.

Amble, St Cuthbert

St Cuthbert's was built in 1870 to a design by Austin and Johnson of Newcastle – a small stone building in Early Decorated style. The choir vestry was added in 1929. The organ was installed in 1876. There is Victorian glass in the windows on the south and north walls. The east window was dedicated in 1928.

The west window was added in 1970 to celebrate the church's centenary. It symbolically depicts aspects of St Cuthbert's life. New glass in the window in the south sanctuary wall, a gift of Amble Mothers' Union, will show King Egfred and Bishop Trumwine pleading with Cuthbert to agree to become a bishop.

Bolton Chapel

A chapel of ease in the parish of Edlingham. It is mentioned in 1230 and although some early work survives, including a twelfth-century chancel arch, it was substantially restored in the nineteenth century.

Boulmer, St Andrew

A simple structure built in 1881 to serve as both church and schoolroom.

Chevington, St John

The nave was built in local black dolerite in 1858 on land given by Earl Grey. The chancel and choir vestry were added in 1893. The altar rail, clergy and choir stalls were installed in 1958 to celebrate the church's centenary. The two-manual organ (1902) is by Harrison and Harrison.

Craster, St Peter the Fisherman

A simple church built in sandstone and slate in 1877. It includes glass by Ruskin and by Leonard Evetts. The gable cross of the east end is a recent addition.

Denwick Church

This simple stone church is described by Pevsner as 'a plain little rectangle with lancet windows'. It was built in 1872.

Edlingham, St John the Baptist

St John's is thought to date back to the eighth century. Eleventh-century work may survive in the west wall but the main part of present building is from the twelfth century. The north arcade was added in about 1190. The substantial tower with its slit windows was added in the fourteenth century. It may have also served as a refuge, like a pele tower. The tomb of Sir William de Felton of nearby Edlingham castle, who died in 1358, is in the church. The north aisle was rebuilt in the fifteenth century. The south porch was probably added in the seventeenth century. Sash windows were inserted in the eighteenth century and a vestry built in the nineteenth century. The building was restored in 1902 by Plummer.

Embleton, Holy Trinity

Holy Trinity was probably first built in the twelfth or early thirteenth century. Further building took place in the fifteenth century but it was substantially remodelled in the nineteenth century. The west bays of the aisle are the work of John Dobson in 1850, and in 1867 F.R. Wilson replaced the chancel and re-roofed the nave. A peal of six bells was hung in the late nineteenth century and the Harrison and Harrison organ was built in 1906. There is some striking glass by Kempe (1884) and more recently by Evetts. A late twentieth-century sculpture of the Holy Trinity is placed over the main door.

Felton, St Michael and All Angels

St Michael's was consecrated in 1199, the gift of William Bertram II, the grandson of the founder of Brinkburn Priory. Two main periods of construction can be seen – from about 1200 and then the later fourteenth century (including the aisles). There is also evidence of some later thirteenth-century work. The earlier work is in the chancel and nave. There is a fourteenth-century effigy of a priest set into the floor of the north aisle. There were various stages of restoration, extension and rebuilding in about 1845, 1870, 1884 and 1900.

Glanton, St Peter

A very simple wooden structure built in 1891 and destroyed by fire on 11 March 2005.

Hepple, Christ Church

Christ Church was designed in local stone by J. Hodgson Fowler in late Perpendicular style. It was built by Jackson of Newcastle in 1893-4. The font bowl may be Saxon or perhaps (and according to Pevsner) post-Conquest. It was found at 'Kirkfield' on West Hepple Farm, where the remains of an ancient chapel were removed in 1760. A grave cover from the site, as well as a cross fragment found on the moors above Hepple, are preserved in the church.

Holystone, St Mary the Virgin

The simple Victorian stone church of St Mary's stands on the site of a former Augustinian priory, probably founded in the twelfth century. Few traces of this remain. What did was largely demolished in 1848-9 when the church was rebuilt in Romanesque style by G. Pickering, but there are traces of early masonry in the south wall of the choir and in the nave, which is said to have been built on the foundations of the medieval choir. A blocked doorway to the right of the present west door is also twelfth-century. Medieval gravestones are set into the south wall of the choir. The Victorian glass is by Wailes and Strang. On the north side of the nave there is a fine Millennium window presented to the church by the people of Holystone. It was designed and manufactured by Jan and Dawn Watson of Harbottle Grange and dedicated in 2002.

The well on the south side of the village, now known as the 'Lady's well', is said to be the site at which early Northumbrian saints including Kentigern (alias Mungo) and Paulinus preached and baptized in the sixth and seventh centuries.

Howick, St Michael and All Angels

St Michael's may possibly have a Saxon origin, but was completely rebuilt in 1746 in Classical style by Sir Henry Grey and then restored and enlarged (a chancel and vestry were added) in Romanesque style by F.J. Francis for the Third Earl Grey in 1849. The two-manual organ was built by Harrison and Harrison in 1931.

There is a group of probably thirteenth-century grave-covers in the churchyard.

The tomb of Charles, the Second Earl Grey, author of the Great Reform Bill of 1832, lies in the church.

The church is situated in the grounds of Howick Hall, within Howick Gardens, one of the loveliest woodland gardens open to the public in the North of England.

Lesbury, St Mary

St Mary's may have Saxon origins, but the earliest surviving stonework and layout of the nave may date to the twelfth century as maybe the lower part of the tower. The chancel shows thirteenth- and fourteenth-century phases and has a fine late medieval roof. The south wall and porch date from a major restoration of the building in 1849 by Anthony Salvin. The font is fifteenth-century and bears the arms of the Percy family. Paintings include the arms of King George III and, from c.1850, Commandment, Creed and Lord's Prayer boards. The two-manual organ by Nicholson and Newbegin was installed in 1908.

Longframlington, St Mary the Virgin

Walter de Framlington is said to have built St Mary's in about 1190, although there is some evidence that fragments of older work were incorporated into the late twelfth-century building. The chancel was substantially restored in 1882 by John Wardle, and the nave in 1896 by Hicks and Charlewood, but the Romanesque chancel arch survives, with three detached pillars on each side. The similarity of the style of this to work at Brinkburn Priory suggests that it may be the work of the same builders.

Longhoughton, St Peter and St Paul

This church was probably built in the eleventh century and retains some early features including the chancel arch and the piers of the tower arch. It was enlarged in the twelfth century – the south aisle is in Transitional style and a window is of the same date. It was restored in 1873 by Streatfield.

The tower (apart from the top which was rebuilt after a fire in about 1840) is also early. The walls of the lower half of it, over 1m thick, witness to its function as a place of refuge or defence.

A small cross in the churchyard (a little over 1m high) may be of pre-Conquest or perhaps of early medieval date. It is probably a grave-marker.

Newton by the Sea, St Mary the Virgin

A simple mission church built about 1870 in corrugated iron with a timbered interior.

Rennington, All Saints

The present church was built in 1831 but is on the site of an early medieval building. It is in Early English style. The interior was entirely restored and enlarged in 1865, when the richly decorated chancel was built. Another source dates the main build to 1837 and the restoration to 1880. The octagonal font is fourteenth-century and was formerly in Embleton Church.

Rock, St Philip and St James

Originally a late twelfth-century building, of which only the lower part of the west front of the church, the chancel arch and a considerable part of the north and south walls survive from that date, along with a late twelfth-century cross-slab set into the chancel floor. The church was ruinous by the seventeenth century and was largely rebuilt by Charles Bosanquet in 1806. Further substantial work took place in 1855 (by Salvin) and again in 1866 (by F.R. Wilson) when the north aisle was built to house an imposing (Pevsner says 'oversized') organ by Grey and Davison, to a design by Holford Bosanquet, who gave the instrument to the church. The apse is also nineteenth-century. There is some glass by Evetts.

Rothbury, All Saints

All Saints may lie on the site of a very substantial early church. A dowsing survey by Denis Briggs suggests monastic buildings extended a considerable distance to the west of the present church. The church seems to have been rebuilt in the thirteenth century and the chancel arch and two arches on the north side of the choir and the piscina to the south of the altar are now the main remnants. The church was largely rebuilt in 1850 by G. Pickering. The vestry was added in 1887 and the south porch in 1929.

The glass is mostly Victorian, but that in the memorial chapel in the south transept is by Leonard Evetts. The chancel screen was erected in 1900 in memory of Lord Armstrong.

Three medieval grave-covers are built into the wall of the outer porch, but the chief glory of All Saints is the pedestal of the font, which once formed part of an early Anglo-Saxon cross, probably dating from the late eighth or the first half of the ninth century. On the north side of this cross shaft can be seen the earliest English representation of the Ascension. Some very fine scrollwork, representations of beasts and perhaps also a scene of the damned in hell can also be seen. The shaft was pressed into service as a font pedestal in 1664 (the date of the bowl), but the head of the cross was found during the 1850 building work. It may now be seen in the Museum of Antiquities in Newcastle upon Tyne. It is the oldest surviving rood in England – the arms of the crucified Christ form the arms of the cross.

Shilbottle, St James

The present St James's was designed in 'Late Decorated' style by W.S. Hicks and reopened in 1885 (it closely resembles Hick's work at Blyth, St Cuthbert). It stands on the site of a smaller medieval building, from which survive the (re-sited) Romanesque chancel arch, the porch doorway, two small windows in the north wall and the font. The east window is the village war memorial placed here in 1921. Glass in a small window in the south transept is by Kempe. The ceilings are a particularly beautiful feature of the church, with the symbols of the Passion shown decorating the area beneath the tower.

Thropton, St Andrew

St Andrew's, with its rough-cast, white-washed walls was built by public subscription in 1900-2 on land donated by Lord Armstrong of Cragside. The pews were brought from St Barnabas, Thorneyford near Ponteland in 1973.

Warkworth, St Lawrence

A church is said to have stood on this site since at least 737 when Ceowulf, king of Northumbria, gave 'Wercewode' and its church of St Lawrence to the abbot and monks of Holy Island. The foundations of a later Saxon church have been traced beneath the present chancel arch, where a small cross marks the place where the altar stood.

The present St Lawrence's is a very fine large post-Conquest, Romanesque building. As such it is, as Pevsner remarks, unique in Northumberland. It soon witnessed tragedy: within its walls on 13 July 1174 Duncan, Earl of Fife, accompanying the Scottish King William the Lion, put to death three hundred of the inhabitants of the town who had taken refuge there. The nave is the longest Romanesque example in Northumberland. The spacious south isle was built by the Percys in the fifteenth century. The beams of the original lead roof remain, but the floor beneath of Caithness stone was laid recently. The vestry is also fifteenth-century and may once have been an anchorite's dwelling. The parvise above the porch, once a curate's lodging, has also served as a school.

The church was in a ruinous state by the mid-nineteenth century and was restored in 1860-1 by Dobson. Further work took place in the chancel in the 1920s and in the south aisle in 1947.

Fragments of medieval glass can be seen in the east window of the south aisle; there is also much Victorian and some modern glass. The pulpit contains some beautiful panels, the work of a modern artist, Alfred Southwick.

Monuments in the church include a very fine figure of a recumbent knight and fragments of early decorated stonework including a very early Celtic cross-head, now in the chancel, and in the baptistry is the gravestone of William Baker, emissary of Queen Margaret of Anjou. The royal arms by the font are of James II and bear the date 1685. Early medieval stone coffins rest against the outside wall of the chancel.

Famous residents of Warkworth include Harry Hotspur. Visitors include the Old Pretender, who was proclaimed King James III at Warkworth market cross on 9 October 1715, after attending Morning Prayer at St Lawrence's (the Vicar refused to pray for him), and Charles Wesley, who preached to a 'quiet and attentive congregation' here in 1761.

Whittingham, St Bartholomew

Whittingham boasts one of the finest Saxon towers in Northumberland. The lower part of this, together with the arch into the tower and part of the wall of the north aisle of the church, is said to date to about 900, but a church was consecrated here as early as 735, and in 684 a religious assembly had taken place at Whittingham for the election of Cuthbert of Lindisfarne as bishop.

The twelfth, thirteenth and fourteenth centuries all saw changes to the architecture of the church. A north aisle and arcade were built in the twelfth century. During the thirteenth century the existing south aisle with an arcade of octagonal pillars was added. The porch is probably fourteenth-century. In 1840 the square Saxon top of the tower was destroyed and replaced with a taller one with pinnacles, and a copy of the thirteenth-century south arcade replaced the earlier north arcade. In 1871 the chancel of 1730 was replaced by F.R. Wilson with a higher one, a pointed arch entrance and a decorative east window.

Impressive features of St Bartholomew's interior are the six exceptionally well-preserved hatchments hanging within the church. These are black-edged, six-foot, diamond-shaped paintings representing heraldic insignia. They date from 1784 to 1855.

A plain medieval stone cross stands near the eastern gate of the churchyard.

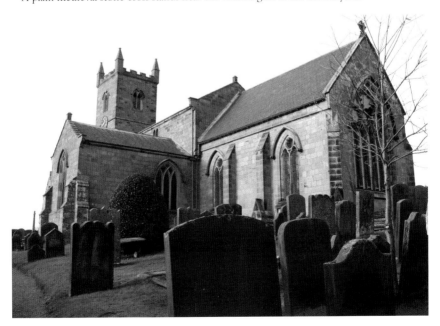

BAMBURGH AND GLENDALE DEANERY

Bamburgh, St Aidan

There are no traces of the original wooden church Bede described as built outside the castle wall by Aidan in 635 (other than a beam now incorporated in the baptistry roof, traditionally believed to be the beam against which Aidan leant as he died). A monument in the chancel, however, records the death of Aidan on that spot in 652.

There is some small evidence of a pre-Conquest stone structure. A few traces of stonework remain in the eastern wall of the north transept.

Towards the end of the twelfth century the church was rebuilt in its present form by the Augustinian canons of Nostell Priory in Yorkshire. The chancel, unusually large for its time, was added in about 1230, and there were many modifications and extensions in the succeeding centuries. Much repair and maintenance work was carried out in 1830, including the replacement of the wooden roofs of the nave and aisles, and then in 1895 by W.S. Hicks.

Beneath the sanctuary and chancel, but only accessible from outside, is a crypt. It was used for many years as a burial chamber.

Between the chancel and the south transept there is a fine 'squint'. The north transept was originally a chantry endowed by Thomas de Bamburgh in 1333. In 1985 this was reordered and dedicated as a chapel in honour of Oswald, King and Martyr.

The elaborate reredos was built of Caen stone in 1895 by Hicks. It depicts northern saints of the seventh and eighth centuries. There are four funeral hatchments above the nave arcades, three dedicated to members of the Forster family, one to the first Lord Armstrong. Most of the glass is nineteenth century, but includes some seventeenth-century Flemish work in the chancel. There are also two distinctive 1936 windows by J.M. Ballantyne. The two-manual Harrison and Harrison organ built in 1883 was restored in 1996. Two eighteenth-century bells were incorporated into the present peal of eight between 1907 and 1912.

Grace Darling, the young girl who took part in the rescue of men from the S.S. Forfarshire in 1842, was born in Bamburgh. Her family grave is in the churchyard, as is the recently refurbished (2004) memorial dedicated to her and originally built in 1844 by Raymond Smith.

The huge churchyard offers magnificent views over the sea to Holy Island.

Beadnell, St Ebba

The first chapel at Beadnell was built perhaps as early as the seventh century on a rocky point near the harbour known now as Ebb's Nook. Ruins on the site date, however, from the thirteenth century. A new chapel replaced it on the site of the present St Ebba's, but this too was rebuilt in 1746, a simple structure without a chancel, but with a gallery as the west end. It was enlarged in 1792 by William Athey and again in 1860 by F.R. Wilson, when it was largely rebuilt and given Gothic style windows along with the charming spire with its unusual pierced octagonal stone screen around its foot.

There is glass by Hatten, Slater and Wailes. The most recent glass, by J.E. Nuttygens, is a memorial window to the men of the village who died in the Second World War.

Belford, St Mary

Records show that there was a church on the site by about 1100. The first stone building dates to about 1200. A Romanesque chancel arch survives. It was repaired and altered extensively in 1615 (the date of the chancel door), 1700 and then by John Dobson in 1828-9. The porch was added in 1844 and the gallery was converted to form a meeting room in 1965.

There is glass by Kempe (1887 and 1902) and the two-manual organ built by Blackett and Howden (Newcastle) in 1906 was fully restored in 1975. A Hanoverian coat of arms is in the porch.

There is a watch-tower in the south-west corner of the graveyard – presumably a precaution against grave robbers who wished to supply the medical schools of Edinburgh with cadavers (see also Doddington, below).

In the churchyard the passage of migrant birds in spring and autumn can be seen. These include redstarts and pied and red-breasted flycatchers. Regular winter visitors include waxwings and bramblings. There are breeding tree sparrows and tawny owls. Among the reptiles are slow-worms and occasionally grass snakes. The main, non-human mammalian life is a churchyard cat (black and white) called Henry.

Chatton, Holy Cross

The original church building at Chatton was granted to Alnwick Abbey between 1157-1184 by the Norman Baron of Alnwick, William de Vesci. It is thought that the monks of Alnwick used to spend the summer months at Chatton. After the Dissolution of the Monasteries the patronage was vested in the Earldom of Percy. It is believed that the first church was destroyed in the thirteenth century; a second church on a site nearer to the river was subjected to flooding and burned down early in the eighteenth century – though the walls survived. The vicar, William Burrell, started restoration work, though the place is reported to have been in ruins for many years and possibly afflicted by another fire. Rebuilding started in earnest in 1770 in the early Gothic Revival style. The north aisle was added by Salvin in 1846 and other work was carried out in 1896.

The organ, which is still in use each Sunday, is a rare piece by G.M. Holdich, and was formerly housed in Trinity College, Oxford. It is possibly one of the oldest organs in the county of Northumberland.

Chillingham, St Peter

As well as twelfth and thirteenth-century stonework in the nave, there are fourteenth and sixteenth-century windows, a sixteenth-century 'king-post' nave roof, a Jacobean pulpit, a font of 1670, a bellcote of 1753 and box pews installed in 1829. The chancel arch dates from a restoration in 1828 by Wyatville.

The sanctuary was completely refurbished in 1967, and a millennium plaque recognises that Christian worship has been offered on this site for over 1000 years.

Perhaps the most significant monument here is the famous fifteenth-century tomb of Sir Ralph Grey and his wife Elizabeth, sited in the South Chapel.

Doddington, St Mary and St Michael

The present building is said to be built on the site of a thirteenth-century church. It was largely rebuilt in 1838 by Ignatius Bonomi, with a new chancel and a new wall to the north aisle. Further changes, by George Reavell, took place in 1893. Most unusually, the church faces west, and not east, with the chancel at the west end.

Two medieval gravestones are in the porch. The 1826 watch-tower in the corner of the churchyard was built to guard against body-snatchers (see also Belford, above).

Eglingham, St Maurice

The first church here may date from the ninth century or earlier (King Coelwulf granted Eglingham to Lindisfarne Priory in 738) but little or nothing of the original building remains. The tower is probably thirteenth-century. Like a number of others in the county, it may also have served as a refuge in troubled times. Most of the church was rebuilt in the seventeenth century (it had been sacked by the Scots in 1596). The vestry was added in 1828, the north porch in 1865 and finally the spire late in the nineteenth century.

The octagonal font is dated 1663. Beneath the chancel floor is a vault containing the remains of members of the Collingwood family (relatives of Admiral Collingwood, Nelson's second-in-command at Trafalgar). A new window featuring the Northumbrian countryside was dedicated in 2001.

The churchyard is managed in a wildlife-friendly way.

Ellingham, St Maurice

There has been a church on this site since at least 1150, possibly earlier. The present church was built by the Revd Charles Thorp in 1862 (Pevsner says to the designs of the Revd J.F. Turner), to replace an earlier 1805 church which collapsed completely. It was built in Early English style, a simple cruciform, with a very high roof ridge. There are three survivals of earlier churches of uncertain date – a piscina in the south wall of the sanctuary, a lancet window in the east wall of the south transept and a font bowl at the front of the nave. In the churchyard are three sandstone pinnacles from the tower of the 1805 church. Extensive repairs to the roof and tower interior were undertaken in 2004.

There may be some seventeenth-century Flemish glass in the east window, but most of the glass is nineteenth century and mostly in the form of memorials to members of the Baker Cresswell family. The fine windows in the north and south transepts depict the *Benedicite* and *Te Deum*. The window on the south side of the nave is of particular interest. It shows (with their dates!) the building of Noah's Ark, the Temple in Jerusalem, Durham Cathedral and Ellingham Church – unified by a central panel depicting Christ the carpenter. The two-manual organ by Gray and Davidson of London was built in 1871 and is unmodified, except for the addition of an electric blower.

Ilderton, St Michael

The church of St Michael, erected on the site of an older building, was largely rebuilt in the late eighteenth century. Only parts of the tower and tower arch appear to date to the thirteenth century. It was repaired and re-roofed in 1851. It was again restored and reseated in 1879, when the chancel was also richly decorated. The font is dated 1727.

A chalice from St Michael's dated 1583 is said to be the only piece of Newcastle silver to survive from the Elizabethan era.

Ingram, St Michael and All Angels

St Michael's was probably founded before the Norman Conquest, but little of this early church survives. In the fourteenth century it boasted north and south chantry chapels, wide aisles and a long chancel. However, it fell into disrepair and was substantially restored in the 1870s as a memorial to the wife and sons of James Allgood, the then rector, who had been killed in a railway accident. The tower was rebuilt in 1905. There is glass by Heaton, Butler and Bayne and by Powell. The fittings (including altar and pulpit) were installed in 1911-2 by Hicks and Charlewood.

The lych-gate was erected in 1928.

Kirknewton, St Gregory the Great

Stonework in the north-west corner of the chancel and coffin lids reused in the north and south walls of the tower may be Saxon. The superb though rather rustic carving of the adoration of the magi, now on the facing wall of the chancel arch above the priest's stall, is of disputed date (the magi seem to be wearing kilts!). It is most probably from the twelfth century, but a ninth-century date has also been suggested.

Most of what now survives from the early medieval period is from the thirteenth century, the date at which a north aisle was added to the church (although this does not remain). In the late fifteenth century the present chancel was built to replace an earlier, longer structure. The walls are unusually thick, perhaps to guard against attack. The last major restoration took place between 1856 and 1860 by John Dobson, who produced a nave, porch and north aisle in typical Lancet style. The Perpendicular-style tower was added a little later.

In the graveyard, immediately to the west of the tower, is the grave of the great social reformer Josephine Butler (1828–1906).

Less than a mile from St Gregory's lay Ad-Gefrin, the royal residence of Edwin king of Northumbria. Pope Gregory I sent the monk Paulinus to accompany Edwin's new Kentish Christian wife Ethelburga to the North. In 36 days at Ad-Gefrin Paulinus instructed and baptized converts and baptized them in the River Glen.

Lucker, St Hilda

The present building is the fifth or possibly sixth to have existed on this site and may even have Saxon origins. The present building replaced an eighteenth-century predecessor and was completed in 1874 by George Reavell in sandstone with plain leaded glass and a gentle apse in Early English style. Stained glass was added subsequently in the nave and chancel. It replaced a church described in 1854 as being 'unsafe for man or beast'.

Kestrels have nested in the bell tower, swallows in the porch. Tawny owls nest in the churchyard. Barn owls regularly hunt in adjacent fields. The river Waren runs along the south side of the churchyard and has regular sightings of otters and a kingfisher.

North Sunderland, St Paul

St Paul's was built in 1833-4 to a design by Anthony Salvin on the site of a medieval pele tower. It is in Romanesque style with an apse. There is some fine glass designed by Leonard Evetts, executed by Walker and Milligan in 1950, in the north wall of the nave.

Old Bewick, Holy Trinity

Originally built in the eleventh or twelfth century (the chancel arch and sanctuary windows still survive), Holy Trinity was restored in the fourteenth century after damage by the Scots, and again in the seventeenth century. It was rebuilt in 1866-7 by R. Williams. There is a fourteenth-century effigy in the choir.

The churchyard is managed in a wildlife-friendly way.

South Charlton, St James

Originally built in the thirteenth century, St James's had fallen into disrepair by the eighteenth century and was rebuilt in Early English style in 1862 by James Deason.

Wooler, St Mary

Although a church may have existed here since the twelfth century, the present St Mary's dates from 1764-5, when it replaced an earlier building severely damaged by fire in 1762 and 1763. It was extended in 1826, 1873 (by F.R. Wilson) and then in 1912-3 when the chancel and clergy vestry were built. The fine west window of 1903 is by Percy Bacon and Bros.

MORPETH DEANERY

Ashington, Holy Sepulchre

Holy Sepulchre was built in 1887-96 as a result of an
initiative by the Hon. Revd W.E. Ellis, the vicar of
Bothal, to form a new parish of Ashington. Money
was donated by the Duke of Portland (£500) and
the Ashington Coal Company (£300), on condi-
tion no bell-tower be built lest its employees be kept
awake! The building was designed by W.S. Hicks and
built by William Carse and Son of Amble at a cost
of around £1200. The War memorial at the east end
was inserted in 1923 to a design by Edie Reed.

Bolam, St Andrew

The oldest part of St Andrew's is the very fine pre-Conquest tower, probably built in the eleventh century. The chancel is post-Conquest Romanesque, along with the chancel arch. The
nave, probably built on Saxon foundations, was widened by the addition of an imposing south
aisle with its handsome arcade and its decorative main south door in the later twelfth century.
The tower arch bears some twelfth-century carving on its capitals. In the thirteenth century the
chancel was lengthened in typical Northumbrian style, including a fine triple lancet window in
the new east wall, along with the seat recesses ('sedilia') for clergy use. Finally in the medieval
period, a chapel was built at the east end of the south aisle. In this lies the superb effigy of a
knight, either Robert Raymes, who died in 1323, or his son, also Robert, who died in 1349.

This beautiful church escaped the wholesale 'restoration' suffered by so many in the eighteenth and nineteenth centuries, with the exception of a vestry and a few windows from that time (by F.R. Wilson), and the squeamish removal of grotesque heads carved in the roll moulding of the chancel arch.

In addition to the medieval grave-covers set into the floor of the south aisle there are others built into the porch.

A small window with glass by Leonard Evetts in the chapel's east wall celebrates the church's escape from serious damage in 1942 when it was hit by a bomb that failed to explode.

Bothal, St Andrew

The traditional date for the building of St Andrew's is about 882. Stonework and Anglo-Saxon crosses suggest a date in the tenth or eleventh century. The nave was rebuilt sometime about 1200, or possibly a little earlier, and the chancel, north aisle and south east chapel were added in the thirteenth century. The chapel was then extended in the following centuries and included the fine early sixteenth-century alabaster tomb of Ralph, the third Lord Ogle, and also that of his wife Margaret. Fragments of medieval glass remain in the aisle windows. In the fifteenth century a new, lower roof was built. In 1887 the building was extensively restored; this included the building of the south porch and the rebuilding of the east end of the church.

Cambo, Holy Trinity

The present church was built in 1842 and replaced a chapel probably built in the twelfth or thirteenth century and demolished in 1795. It is in Lancet style and consists of a nave, with a pentagonal eastern apse, and a western tower containing a clock and a peal of 6 bells. The tower was built at the cost of Sir George Trevelyan MP when the church was restored in 1884. In 1965 the interior was reordered, when panelling was removed and new pews were installed. A few early coffin covers are preserved in the wall of the Victorian building.

Cresswell, St Bartholomew

St Bartholomew's was built as an estate chapel and district church within the parish of Woodhorn by the Baker-Cresswell family of Cresswell Hall in about 1836 (and therefore displays the coat of arms of William IV). The interior was reordered in 1947, including a new pulpit as a war memorial to parishioners who died in the Second World War.

There are additional memorial plaques to those who fell in the Great War: to the Revd Robert Taylor (Vicar of Cresswell, drowned off Cresswell beach in 1894) and to Margaret Armstrong (1851-1927), recipient of RNLI Gold Brooch for 50 years service with the Cresswell lifeboat. There is good nineteenth-century glass by Thomas Willement (of about 1836-9) and Joseph Baguley and twentieth-century glass by Leonard Evetts. The late nineteenth-century two-manual organ by Nicholson was refurbished in 1936 and 1999.

Hartburn, St Andrew

St Andrew's was the property of Tynemouth Priory in 1207, but has earlier origins. The tower is late Saxon, perhaps eleventh or twelfth-century. The nave and chancel are mostly mid-thirteenth century. The typical long chancel shows signs of having been extended. The capitals of the columns in the nave carry carvings of fish and animals. The font also seems to date to around 1250. The building is said to have been associated at this time with the Knights Templar. Two daggers and a possible Maltese cross on the doorpost may corroborate this claim (though Pevsner does not discuss this possibility). Restoration in the eighteenth and late nineteenth century did little to spoil the medieval charm of the building. There are two pre-Reformation bells, a reredos and pulpit in Caen stone, introduced in 1890, and a 1942 window by Leonard Evetts.

There are some particularly fine eighteenth-century headstones in the churchyard.

Hebron, St Cuthbert

When the first St Cuthbert's was built at Hebron (Hebburn) is not known, but it was ruinous by 1674 and was rebuilt, largely in 1793, although stonework in the chancel, possibly twelfth century, was preserved along with a fourteenth- or fifteenth-century chancel arch.

Kirkharle, St Wilfrid

St Wilfrid's is a simple but beautiful fourteenth-century building in Decorated style, altered in 1771–8 (when the west gable, porch and bell cope were added by Sir William Loraine) and in 1884. There are three medieval sedilia in the south wall of the chancel and a piscina with a projecting basin. The fifteenth- or sixteenth-century font, which bears the arms on each of its eight sides of old Northumbrian families, was rescued from the medieval church of All Saints, Newcastle.

The great gardener Lancelot (Capability) Brown was born here and baptised in St Wilfrid's on 30 August 1716. There is a monument to him in the nave.

Kirkheaton, St Bartholomew

A medieval church, but only a few stones seem to have survived the rebuilding (paid for by Mrs Dorothy Windsor) in 1755. The bellcote, which probably dates from this time, is described by Pevsner as 'fantastic'. The building was later 'gothicized' in 1866–7.

Kirkwhelpington, St Bartholomew

A thirteenth-century (or possibly earlier) building, St Bartholomew's, with its low, broad Perpendicular tower and long nave and chancel, was altered in the fifteenth century and then in 1896. Excavations have revealed that the building originally had aisles and transepts.

There are two fourteenth-century bells, a seventeenth-century font (which rests on the reversed capital of a fourteenth or fifteenth-century pier) and a mahogany pulpit from 1797. The glass includes work by Heaton, Butler and Bayne (1909 and 1914).

The distinguished engineer and inventor Sir Charles Parsons is buried here with his wife Katherine (there is a memorial to them in the church) and the celebrated antiquary John Hodgson wrote his *History of Northumberland* during his incumbency between 1823–34.

Longhirst, St John the Evangelist

St John's was built in 1876 at a cost of £3950. The architect was Sir Arthur Blomfield. The oak chancel screen is the work of parishioners and the Revd R. Proctor, vicar from 1885 to 1916.

The lych-gate was built in 1885.

Longhorsley, St Helen

A medieval, possibly even Saxon, church stood half a mile south of the village. It was rebuilt in 1783-98 but was abandoned in 1966 and is now ruinous. The congregation adapted the old church school, built in 1848, for use as a church and in 1981 rebuilt the porch from the old church at the west end.

Lynemouth, St Aidan

Originally intended as a church hall but, following the General Strike of 1926, plans for a separate church were abandoned and the hall became a composite church/hall from 1925-59. After the building of a separate hall, the building became a dedicated church, consecrated in 1961 when the conventional district became the parish of Lynemouth. The parish was united with Cresswell in 1971 to form the new parish of Cresswell and Lynemouth. With the sale and eventual demolition of the hall, the church was reordered in 1990 and reverted to multi-purpose use.

Meldon, St John

St John's is a small stone church, the earliest stonework of which appears to be thirteenth century. It was restored in about 1849 by Dobson when the triple lancet window in the east end was probably inserted (the glass is later – by Leonard Evetts). A fine seventeenth-century effigy near the font is that of Sir William Fenwick, a Royalist, who died in London in 1652.

A thirteenth-century cross-slab is in the churchyard near the south door.

Mitford, St Mary Magdalene

St Mary's is a twelfth-century foundation, but all that remains of the mid-twelfth-century church, probably built in two stages, are the pillars on the south side of the nave, the projecting corbel on the south side of the chancel arch and the priest's door on the south side of the chancel. In 1216 St Mary's was burned by King John, with many of the villagers who had taken sanctuary in the church still inside. In 1327 the church was damaged, probably by fire, when the castle was also destroyed. In 1705 the nave roof was yet again destroyed by fire from the open braziers heating the church.

St Mary's was re-roofed and restored in about 1840 and then enlarged in 1870 by R.J. Johnson for the squire of Mitford. A new chancel arch was raised, the chancel repaired and a new east window installed. The old bell-tower at the west end was replaced by a splendid new tower and spire. A new reredos was fitted in 1883. In 1984 the nave and chancel were re-roofed and the woodblock floor replaced by York stone.

The ancient bell now hanging beside the main door is believed to be from the twelfth century and to be the oldest bell in Britain. A peal of 13 bells was hung in 1876, operated from the baptistry by ropes. The two-manual Nicholson organ of 1878 was recently restored. The Mitford window in the south aisle is by Kempe (1895).

There is a fine tomb – of Bertram Reveley, who died in 1625. The lych-gate was built in 1889.

Morpeth, Stobhill, St Aidan

An unpretentious brick building built in the late 1950s.

Morpeth, St James

St James's was built as a town centre church through the initiative and drive of the then Rector, the Honourable and Reverend Francis Richard Grey, who was new to the town. The mother church, St Mary's, on the southern perimeter of the town had become too small to contain the number which would otherwise attend, and was too far from the town to enable the old and infirm to worship. The church was built on land given by the rector's father-in-law, the Earl of Carlisle, upon which he had a town house which he was happy to see demolished to make way for the new church, and by Mrs John Fenwick.

It was designed by Benjamin Ferrey in a Romanesque style similar to the cathedral at Monreale, near Palermo in Sicily, which was built in 1172. The foundation stone was laid on St James's Day, 1844 and the building was completed in 1846. The murals in the apse were painted in 1875 by Clayton and Bell. The choir vestry was added in 1887. Major restoration work on the tower and bell turret was carried out in 1994 by J. and W. Lowry of Newcastle and major conservation work followed on the apse paintings in 2004.

The majority of the glass is by William Wailes but some windows are thought to be the work of Charles Clutterbuck. A window in the Grey Chapel is by Leonard Evetts from about 1946.

The imposing 'Grey Memorial Arches' to the west of the church were erected after the death of Rector Grey in 1890. The avenue of lime trees leading to the west door was planted in the 1880s.

Morpeth, St Mary the Virgin

St Mary's was probably begun in the thirteenth century but is, for the most part, one of the finest and largest fourteenth-century churches in Northumberland. The *Jesse window* – the east window of the chancel – is the chief glory of the church. It is of fourteenth-century glass restored by Wailes (who made the rest of the glass in the chancel), although the south aisle east window has the oldest and most important early fourteenth-century glass in the upper part of the window. Both windows have recently been restored. The priest's door in the chancel retains its original late fourteenth-century hinges. The south porch was added in the sixteenth century. The font is thirteenth century; the screen and pulpit were installed in about 1900.

St Mary's churchyard has a guard hut, built in the 1830s, which was occupied by watchmen to guard the cemetery against grave-robbers. The lych-gate of 1861 is also very fine.

The churchyard is notable in that it contains the grave of Emily Wilding Davison (born 1872), the suffragette who threw herself in front of the king's horse at Epsom on Derby Day, 1913.

Netherwitton, St Giles

St Giles was built (or perhaps rebuilt) by Roger Thornton, Mayor of Newcastle in 1405. The nave was rebuilt in the eighteenth century and the church was repaired again in 1864, and then largely rebuilt in two stages: in 1881 and 1887. Very little of the medieval building appears to remain: the chancel arch and a reused capital and also a thirteenth- or fourteenth-century font.

There is a fine fourteenth-century tomb-effigy in the chancel, possibly of Agnes Thornton.

Newbiggin-by-the-Sea, St Bartholomew

Pevsner records a local tradition that it was the site of a very early church founded by the Lindisfarne community and there is a documentary reference to a chapel at Newbiggin before 1174. The present church of St Bartholomew, which was founded as a chapel of ease to Woodhorn, appears to incorporate a few stones from a twelfth-century building, but dates to the thirteenth and fourteenth centuries. It is built in an extremely dramatic setting on a rocky point to the east of the present village.

Both nave and chancel are surprisingly long and imposing. The two western bays of the nave seem to have been added later – but in the fourteenth century. The chancel, probably rebuilt or extended in about 1300, includes fine lancet windows (those on the south have been extensively restored). The east window is especially fine, with five lights derived from grouped lancets pierced between the heads. The glass was installed in 1950. The tower, at the west end, is also thirteenth-century and is surmounted by a short plain spire – undoubtedly intended also as a mark for seafarers.

After a period of some neglect, the building was repaired and restored in the nineteenth-century, beginning in 1845. The chancel, which had been walled off, was brought back into use and successive new chancel arches were raised in 1845 and 1898 (by W. S. Hicks). In 1914 the north aisle was added. There are four bells rung by a system of levers and a two-manual organ by Nelson of Durham.

There is an impressive collection of mostly thirteenth-century grave-markers and coffin lids within the church. The best are in the north aisle – now the Lady Chapel.

The rocky headland on which the church is set has a variety of coastal flora and is of particular interest to bird-watchers.

Seaton Hirst, St Andrew

A brick building completed and consecrated in 1932. It replaced a 'tin church' of 1905.

Seaton Hirst, St John

A stone church built in 1896, enlarged in 1905 and 1945 and reordered internally in the early 1960s.

Stannington, St Mary

The present fine Victorian Decorated Gothic building was reconsecrated on 31 October, 1871 and is the work of R.J. Johnson. It incorporates some traces of the older building which is said to have been founded in the late twelfth century. These include thirteenth-century capitals in both arcades. Medieval glass in the vestry window was a gift from Sir Matthew White Ridley in 1722. Fine nineteenth-century glass is by Clayton and Bell, Bacon Bros and Kempe.

There are a number of apparently early grave-covers (in the floor under the tower). Pevsner is undecided whether two of these date from the seventh or eighth century or are twelfth- and thirteenth-century copies.

The lych-gate was built in 1893.

Ulgham, St John the Baptist

There has probably been a church on this site since Saxon times – also suggested by a dowsing survey in 1985. Two window heads remain from a successor, probably built around 1100; one on the outside of the west wall and one on the east wall of the north aisle inside. One of these bears fascinating, though rather crude (Pevsner says 'in a style entirely that of children's art'), contemporary carvings of a woman wearing a long skirt, two birds and a man on horseback.

The present building is of local sandstone and was begun in about 1842 and completed in 1863. The roof of the chancel and vestry are covered with Lake District slate and the nave and north aisle are covered with Welsh slate. Glass is by William Wailes and more recently by Leonard Evetts (1990).

There are seventeenth-century headstones in the ancient burial ground surrounding the church and a cross dedicated to John Bolland, the curate of Morpeth and Ulgham, the driving force behind the initial nineteenth-century restoration of the church. The project was completed by the Rector of Morpeth, Francis Grey, who is commemorated in a window of 1891.

Whalton, St Mary Magdalene

St Mary's reveals an almost complete thirteenth-century church interior which developed from a twelfth-century core. The nave is shorter than usual in local thirteenth-century building, but the presence of the tower to the west may have prevented an extension. There is little twelfth-century work remaining: one fragment is a respond at the west end of the north arcade, a massive column with a heavy, square-scalloped capital – and probably the lower section of the tower (although Pevsner believes this to be eleventh-century). The thirteenth-century building, much as the building is today, consisted of nave with north and south aisles, chancel with its own north aisle (a feature also of Corbridge, Lesbury and Rothbury) and tower. It seems to have been built in two stages – the chancel and its aisle being the first, probably soon after 1200. The strange grotesque head on the north hood of the chancel arch may have been carved at an earlier date. In the fourteenth and fifteenth centuries the aisles were heightened and the north chapel (the chancel aisle) widened.

'Churchwarden' windows were inserted in the eighteenth century, but these were later replaced in 1890 by Hicks and Charlewood in roughly fourteenth-/fifteenth-century style.

There are a few medieval grave-covers in the church and three 'ledger stones' (horizontal gravestones) set into the floor of the north aisle recording burials of the Ogle family in 1564, 1566 and 1613. A 1720 'benefaction board' hangs on the north aisle wall and the royal arms of King George III above the east window of the south aisle. The chancel screen was carved by Ralph Hedley in 1891. The 1911 reredos is by Hicks and Charlewood. The tower clock of 1796 has been restored recently.

Widdrington, Holy Trinity

The north aisle arcade is the earliest part of the building. It dates to the late twelfth century (although the original aisle wall was replaced in the nineteenth century). The remainder of the church is a mixture of thirteenth- and fourteenth-century work. It was restored and repaired in the nineteenth century. A thirteenth-century cross-slab is reused as a lintel to the vestry door!

In the north wall of the chancel are two tomb recesses, one of which is surrounded by the coat of arms of the Widdrington family, whose mansion and castle adjoined the church to the east.

The two-manual organ was built by Blackett and Howden of Newcastle in 1893 and rebuilt in 1995.

NORHAM DEANERY

Ancroft, St Anne

St Anne's is one of four churches built by the priory of Holy Island on its estates on the mainland (the others are at Kyloe, Lowick and Tweedmouth). Ancroft is the only one to retain any of the original building. It was built in the twelfth century. Of this there remain the south wall of the nave, the (blocked up) original Romanesque doorway, the bottom section of the tower, the round-headed window in the west wall and the corbel table (the arched stones below the gutter) from the west angle to the east end of the nave. The tower was built in the thirteenth or early fourteenth century and is unusual in that it is an imposing pele tower attached to the church. Holy Island can be seen from the top. The church was restored in 1836 and then enlarged and further restored in 1870 by F.R. Wilson.

A little to the west of the tower is a headstone marking the graves of eight English Poor Clare nuns who escaped from Rouen during the French Revolution and were given shelter at Haggerston Castle under the protection of Sir Carnaby Haggerston.

Berwick, Holy Trinity

Pevsner declares Holy Trinity to be a building 'of quite exceptional architectural interest'. The first record of a church here dates from 1152 but the present building was built in 1650-2 to a design by John Young of Blackfriars, London by the then Governor, Colonel George Fenwicke, the father-in-law of Oliver Cromwell. It is one of the very few seventeenth-century churches in England and the only parish church to be built during the Commonwealth. Curiously, it has no tower – one was included in the original plan, but it was omitted at Cromwell's request.

It was restored in 1855 when a short chancel was added and some windows were replaced, but its Classical design was not compromised. The fine seventeenth-century arcade with five bays of Tuscan columns and round arches is unaltered. Of the four original galleries only the western one remains.

The reredos is by Sir Edwin Lutyens. There are medallions of fine sixteenth- or seventeenth-century Flemish glass set in the otherwise nineteenth-century glass of the west window in the nave and a new window was recently installed to mark the millennium.

In 1989 a major programme of restoration work was begun to preserve this unique architectural treasure.

Branxton, St Paul

There has been a church at Branxton since at least the twelfth century. Many of the dead from the battle of Flodden Field which took place immediately to the south of the church on 9 September 1513 are said to have been laid here. Only the thirteenth-century chancel arch remains from the medieval building. St Paul's was almost entirely rebuilt in Romanesque style in 1849.

The late seventeenth-century altar rails are made from timber salvaged from a ship which foundered off the Farne Isles.

Carham, St Cuthbert

An ancient church existed here, possibly as early as the late seventh century (two tenth-century cross-shafts are in the Museum of Antiquities in Newcastle), but whatever remained, it was pulled down before the present St Cuthbert's was built in 1790. It was altered and extended in 1862-4 (Pevsner says in 1870) and in 2004 when the tower was rebuilt.

Cornhill-on-Tweed, St Helen

St Helen's is said to be built upon an ancient religious site. It was established as a chapel of ease for Norham in the twelfth century but by 1750 had fallen into disrepair. Rebuilding was completed in 1752. It was heavily modified in 1840 by Ignatius Bonomi and in 1866 when the chancel was built, probably by F.R. Wilson, and the campanile bell-tower was added in 1909.

Etal, St Mary the Virgin

St Mary's was built by Lady Augusta FitzClarence in 1856-8 to the design of William Butterfield as a mortuary chapel in the grounds of Etal Manor for her husband Lord Frederick FitzClarence (illegitimate son of the Duke of Clarence, later King William IV), who died in India in 1854. He, his daughter, Lady Augusta, and Lord Frederick's ADC are buried in the side chapel. The building is one of Butterfield's early works, after Perth Cathedral but well before Rugby School or Keble College. It is built of local pink sandstone banded with light cream ashlars. The chapel consists of a nave and chancel of equal dimensions and a mortuary chapel occupying the place of a south aisle. Butterfield's contemporary furnishing has gone, replaced in 1961 with new light oak choir stalls and pews as a memorial to Lt the Hon. Hugh Joicey, who was killed in action in the Second World War. The cross, altar candlesticks and standing candles to Butterfield's design remain, as does the ironwork at the communion rail and chancel step. The roof over the sanctuary area is decorated with eight-pointed gold flaming stars in a blue background.

Ford, St Michael and All Angels

St Michael's was first built in the thirteenth century and predates the castle in whose grounds it now stands. Only the west wall and the south arches and pillars survive a heavy restoration in Early English style by Dobson in 1853. The 1892 reredos is by Hicks, as is the pulpit.

Two gravestones now inside the church are of particular interest: one is of a tailor, the earlier however, which may date from the fourteenth century, appears to depict the Northumbrian bagpipes.

Holy Island, St Mary the Virgin

It is often claimed, but probably impossible to prove, that St Mary's church stands on the site of the monastery established on the island by St Aidan in the seventh century. The present church is certainly rather confused architecturally. There are additions from almost every age since at least the twelfth century. In the wall that divides the nave from the chancel there is a Saxon arch touching the later Early English arch and high above this a typical Saxon door. On the outside of the building looking west, possible Saxon quoin stones can be seen where the nave joins the chancel. The arches of the church are a mixture of rounded Romanesque and pointed Decorated and it seems that the shape of the church as we see it today was completed by the thirteenth century. St Mary's was restored in 1860 by F.R. Wilson and in 1890 a 'porch' was built on the north as a mortuary for victims of shipwrecks.

In the sanctuary there is a beautiful Celtic carpet made by the women of the island – a copy of the St Mark's Carpet page from the *Lindisfarne Gospels*. A carpet replicating the St Matthew's page was manufactured more recently for the fishermen's altar to celebrate the millennium.

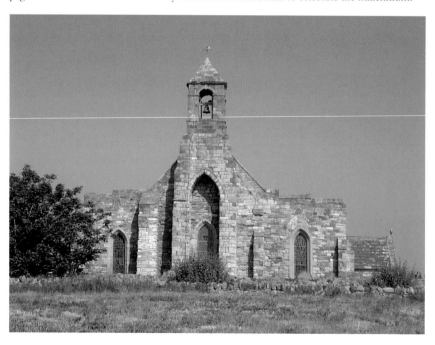

Lowick, St John the Baptist

There has been a church building in Lowick for many centuries. The first church was built before 1145; in that year the
Pope Eugenius III confirmed that Lowick Church belonged
to the Benedictine monks of Holy Island Priory.

The medieval church was demolished in 1794 and a new
church was consecrated in 1796. Like its predecessor this is also
small; just 60 x 25ft, and it was built on the same site. It was
designed by Henry Penny Selby Morton – there is a commem-
orative stone over the entrance. The chancel was built by F.R.
Wilson and the present hammerbeam roof added in 1887.

Norham, St Cuthbert

There was a Saxon church at Norham from 830 (to the east of the present church). St
Ceolwulf is said to have been buried in the porch of that church and St Cuthbert's body was
brought to it in 875.

The present imposing, mostly Romanesque, building is thought to have been built
between 1165 and 1170 by the same architect responsible for the nearby castle. Masons' marks
on an arch are curiously similar to those in Trondheim Cathedral.

The building was altered in 1338-9 (at the east end); in 1617 (a general restoration plus the
tower and porch); on substantial scale in 1837-46 by Ignatius Bonomi (who again rebuilt the
tower, porch and the south aisle); in 1852 by D. Gray (the north aisle) and finally in 1883 (the
north transept).

The oak pulpit is seventeenth century and was brought from Durham Cathedral in 1840.
Stones with Celtic decoration, possibly from the first church, are displayed near the font. A
fourteenth-century tomb of a crusader is now on the south side of the chancel.

The two-manual organ by James J. Binns (Leeds) was installed in 1895-7. There is some good nineteenth-century glass by various artists including Baguley, Bryans, Clayton and Bell and Wailes.

Edward I came here in 1292 to receive homage from John Balliol and other contenders for the Scottish throne.

In 1320 the church was occupied by Robert Bruce during his attack on the castle. Ancient yews to the east of the church grow on the presumed site of the Saxon church.

Scremerston, St Peter

St Peter's was built in 1842-3 by Bonomi and Cory in Early English style. It has an aisleless nave, chancel and a broach spire.

Spittal, St John the Evangelist

St John's is a mid-Victorian sandstone church built in 1869-71. It was originally in primrose sandstone with rose sandstone window and door surrounds but is now blackened. A new high altar integral with a war memorial was introduced in 1921.

Complete internal restoration in 2000 included the conversion of the south aisle into meeting rooms, kitchen and a toilet. The pulpit and choir stalls were also removed.

The organ was installed by Julian Bonia in 2002. It came originally via Ladykirk, then Scremerston Methodist Chapel and then St Cuthbert's, Norham! A new stained-glass window was commissioned for the patrons, the Mercers Company, and installed in 2005.

Tweedmouth, St Bartholomew

The earliest church at Tweedmouth is said to have been destroyed by Viking raiders in 870. A church is thought to have stood on the present site since 1145, but the building that can be seen today dates mostly from 1783. A transept was added in 1841, when F.R. Wilson 'gothicized' the building and rebuilt the chancel in 1866. One window is by Kempe (1887). The church was again restored in 1903-6.

There are Elizabethan headstones in the churchyard.

OTHER CHURCHES OF NOTE

These are no longer used regularly for Anglican worship but are of outstanding architectural or historical interest.

Brinkburn Priory (St Peter and St Paul)

Founded by Augustinian canons between 1130-35, Brinkburn is a fine example of the transition between Romanesque (Norman) style and Early English of around the late twelfth and early thirteenth centuries. It enjoys a fabulous setting beside the River Coquet. It was restored (from ruins) in 1858-9 by Thomas Austin.

Now in the care of English Heritage – but occasional services are still held here, as well as a music festival of international repute.

Bywell, St Andrew

The second major Saxon church in Bywell and, according to Pevsner, the finest Saxon tower in the county of Northumberland, which probably dates to around 1000. The church itself was altered in 1830, in 1850 by John Dobson and in 1871 by William Slater.

Newcastle, All Saints

Although All Saints was deconsecrated in 1961 it fully merits inclusion here because it is a very fine example of late eighteenth-century architecture. It was built in 1786-96 by David Stephenson and enjoys a prominent place on the Newcastle skyline.

Woodhorn, St Mary

An ancient church which has traces of pre-Conquest stonework as well as that of the twelfth and thirteenth centuries. It was heavily restored by John and Benjamin Green in 1842-3. It has served more recently as a museum.

APPENDIX

EILEEN MCLEAN

This is a personal view on how churches can make themselves more accessible and welcoming. Eileen McLean is Vicar of Bamburgh and Ellingham, part of one of the most beautiful stretches of the Northumberland coast and a popular destination for many visitors. (Editor)

HOW TO MAKE A CHURCH WELCOMING

This gazetteer describes many church buildings, all valued and loved within their communities, some exceptionally historic and beautiful. All of these churches are visited by people from outside their worshipping congregation. Some attract many tourists; all churches have visitors at weddings and baptisms and funerals. A very large proportion of these visitors are non-churchgoers.

Churches are places of faith. That is why they were built, to worship God and to draw people closer to God. When visitors come into a church – because they are interested in its history, or because it is a dry place out of the rain, or to enjoy themselves at a friend's wedding – this provides an opportunity to engage with it.

On a recent period of Sabbatical leave I visited 100 churches in various parts of England, all of which attract a large number of tourists. In each one I asked myself: what does this building say to a casual visitor? Does it seem like a museum, confirming prejudices about the Church as an out-of-date and irrelevant institution or does it feel alive and active, with a special sense of sacredness, which may inspire 'why' and 'what' questions?

I tried to bear in mind that many people today have rarely worshipped in a church and know almost nothing of the Christian story. Some will be influenced by a modern spirituality that might involve candles, aromatherapy and meditative music.

I asked myself, what impression does a church building make on such modern non-church-going people? There must be ways, at the very least, of disturbing not confirming existing prejudices, at best, of sparking some imagination and interest in what the church is about.

I began with the premise that every church could try to convey three important messages to its visitors:

1. We are glad you are here; this place is for you.
2. This is not just a beautiful old building, it is a *sacred* space however *you* may understand that word 'sacred'.
3. This church is alive, loved and used regularly by people who follow the way of Christ.

I offer some reflections on my findings:

WHAT KIND OF WELCOME?

A feeling of being welcomed is important. The absence of welcome, or a tainted welcome, will almost certainly discourage people from visiting.

A too-talkative 'steward', an instant request for money, 'keep off' and 'do not' signs – all produce negative feelings. A dark and dusty building, old and faded literature; these are uninviting. Welcome signs lost in a welter of parish notices are useless. Visitors' leaflets which contain Church 'jargon' words are off-putting and excluding.

Conversely, just the word 'open' at the church gate, or 'welcome' in the porch with a vase of flowers – these say 'we hope you will come in'. Well-presented literature, sensor lighting, quiet music (where appropriate) all contribute to a good experience. Imaginative ideas like 'help yourself to coffee' or dog bowls outside the door show generosity of spirit. It's good to see 'Peace be with you' or 'Thank you for visiting' on the exit door.

DOES THE CHURCH BUILDING FEEL LIKE A SACRED SPACE?

Every church is a sacred space, that is what it is for. Regular worshippers know this, and whenever they enter a strange church sacred memories flood back from other times and places. This will not be so for the many visitors who come primarily to explore an ancient and interesting building.

Can a visit to a church building convey something of the sacred, and enable these visitors to get in touch with a spiritual part of themselves?

Sacred ambience
Some church buildings instantly feel sacred. Even the most secular of people are likely to experience these as 'special' places, that produce a sense of awe and wonder and peace. Of course some churches are particularly blessed in their setting, architecture and artefacts. But even these can be diminished, and some very 'ordinary' buildings can be enhanced by a few very simple factors. Clutter and noise tends to obscure the spiritual. Many churches are repositories for old bits of furniture, covered with out-of-date newspapers, ladders, flower-stands etc. These distractions at ground level tend to obscure the ambient spiritual glory.

Noise levels vary greatly in similar churches. In some, where visitors speak and move quietly; tranquillity and a sense of the sacred are preserved. In others, where voices are raised and there is almost an atmosphere of the market-place. The example and expectations of the 'staff' would appear very influential here. Guides talking loudly, clergy rushing around, these encourage noise levels to rise to the detriment of sacred space.

Church buildings as places of prayer and reflection
Believers want to pray in churches they visit. Many others need to find places for quietness and reflection. Churches deliberately engender a sense of prayerfulness in various ways:

Prayers at the entrance
If these are amidst motley notices, they are unnoticed and ineffective – and it seems as though prayer is not taken very seriously.

Quiet prayer chapels

If these are just a bleak space they offer little in the way of help or comfort. Chapels which have icons, candles, prayer cards, meditations, Bibles – those which are imaginatively arranged – are ones in which a person can find serenity and peace.

Candlestands

These are very popular. Often the symbolism is explained and appropriate prayers suggested. Stands thick with old grease are off-putting. Night-lights among pebbles work well.

Prayer request books

If these require explanation and a commitment that the prayers will be offered within worship; they need to be easily visible and a pen must be provided. This is not always the case. Prayer pools offer an imaginative way of praying for others. A pebble representing the person is immersed in a bowl of water; the water representing God's all-surrounding love.

Quietness, rich symbolism and appropriate well thought-out words are the best helps to prayer and reflection, for believer and unbeliever alike.

HOW ARE VISITORS TOLD ABOUT THE CHRISTIAN FAITH?

Very few churches even attempt to do this, although this is an amazing opportunity for the Church to explain its beliefs to those outside its membership. The Church does not need to go *out* to these people. They have voluntarily come *in*. Churches do not appear to seriously consider their buildings as tools of mission. Some churches are producing high-quality leaflets/posters about Christian belief and artefacts used in worship; but even among these, technical terms abound and may not be understood. In a secular age it is a real challenge to present the truths of the Christian faith using comprehensible, attractive and gentle language and imagery.

IS THERE EVIDENCE THAT THIS CHURCH BUILDING IS THE HOME OF AN ACTIVE CHRISTIAN COMMUNITY, INVOLVED IN ITS NEIGHBOURHOOD AND CONCERNED FOR THE WIDER WORLD?

Notice boards, displays about current interests and parish magazines all join to create an impression, positive or negative. The average visitor will not peruse any of these in detail, so impressions are all.

At worst, if a visitor senses that this is an uncared for building and sees no evidence that anything takes place except Sunday services, they will assume that the church is dying from within. On the other hand, they may instantly feel that this is a cherished building, where things happen.

CONCLUDING THOUGHTS

These then are the questions I had in mind as I visited 100 church buildings, as I tried to put myself in the shoes of a tourist with little faith or none:

Am I welcome and wanted here, or do they just want my money?

Is it a 'special place' which engages me in a spiritual way, if only fleetingly?

Does it say something comprehensible about faith to someone largely ignorant of Christianity?

Is it a place in which I could pause to reflect (or pray), and to which I would happily return?

Is it just a holy museum reflecting a dead past, or does it speak of a living Church community, relevantly engaged with the local community and the wider world?

One visit to a church is unlikely to be a life-changing experience – though it is possible. Visiting several, or many, churches over a period can have a cumulative impact, favourable or otherwise, concerning the places, the people who worship in them, and the faith they hold. Lots of people visit lots of churches. Every church can and does contribute to this collective 'build-up' effect, for good or ill.

It is right, therefore, that churches should seek to impress and inspire visitors with their fascinating history and beautiful architecture. They should be welcoming and accessible to all.

ENDNOTES

INTRODUCTION: A SENSE OF PLACE

1 John Grundy, Grace McCombie, Peter Ryder, Humphrey Welfare and Nikolaus Pevsner, *The Buildings of England: Northumberland* (London, Penguin, 1992). A good general description is also provided by M. Slater, *The Old Parish Churches of Northumberland* (Malvern, Folly Publications, 1997).
2 Richard Taylor, *How to Read a Church* (London, Random House, 2003).
3 Simon Jenkins, *England's Thousand Best Churches* (London, Allen Lane, 1999)
4 According to *Government Planning Policy Guidance 15, Section 3.8*, 'generally the best way of securing the upkeep of historic buildings is to keep them in active use'.
5 English Heritage, *Inspired* (London, 2006), 10.
6 Church Heritage Forum, *Building Faith in our Future* (London, Church House Publishing, 2004), 4.
7 Church Heritage Forum, *Faith in our Future*, 28.
8 I am indebted to Bob Langley, Archdeacon of Lindisfarne, who has contributed much to this section and drew my attention to the issue of social capital.

TWO SPIRITUALITY AND THE MODERN CHURCH

1 David Hay and Kate Hunt, *Understanding the Spirituality of People who don't go to Church,* (Nottingham, 2000). This does not appear to have been published commercially. The copy I have came directly from contacting David Hay, and is loose-bound format. The page numbers here refer to that edition.
2 Hay and Hunt, *Understanding the Spirituality*, 12-13.
3 Hay and Hunt, *Understanding the Spirituality*, 26.
4 Hay and Hunt, *Understanding the Spirituality*, 9.
5 Hay and Hunt, *Understanding the Spirituality*, 19.
6 Church of England, *Common Worship: Services and Prayers for the Church of England* (London, Church House Publishing, 2000), ix.
7 *Common Worship*, ix.
8 Henri Nouwen, *The Return of the Prodigal Son* (London, Darton, Longman and Todd, 1992).
9 John V. Taylor, *The Christlike God* (London, SCM, 1992), 27.
10 Church of England, Archbishop's Commission on Urban Priority Areas, *Faith in the City: a call for action by Church and nation: the report of the Archbishop of Canterbury's commission on Urban Priority Areas* (London, Church House, 1985).
11 Hay and Hunt, *Understanding the Spirituality*, 30.
12 Hay and Hunt, *Understanding the Spirituality*, 42.

THREE SEARCHING FOR IDENTITY: THE SOCIAL, ECONOMIC AND CULTURAL CONTEXT OF NEWCASTLE DIOCESE

1 Bill Lancaster. 'Sociability and the City.' In Robert Colls & Bill Lancaster (eds) *Newcastle upon Tyne: A Modern History* (Chichester, West Sussex, Phillimore & Co. Ltd 2001), 319-40 traces the roots of 'party city' in an antiestablishment sentiment born of ordinary folks' exclusion from civic celebrations and reaching back to the early nineteenth century.

2 Tom Cosh. 'Knowledge as a Basis for Local Competitiveness – A Newcastle Case Study'. *Northern Economic Review*. 32. 2002, 182-9.

3 Organisation for Economic Co-operation and Development. OECD Territorial Reviews: Newcastle. 2006 (www.newcastle.gov.uk viewed 25 July 2006).

4 Northumberland County Council Public Inquiry. *Report of the Foot and Mouth Disease Inquiry Panel*. 25 February 2002 (www.northumberland.gov.uk – viewed 25 July 2006).

5 Mike Barke. 'The People of Newcastle: A Demographic History'. In Robert Colls & Bill Lancaster (eds). *Newcastle upon Tyne: A Modern History* (Chichester, West Sussex, Phillimore & Co. Ltd 2001), 133-66.

6 Veena Soni, Government Office North East. *Ethnicity in the North East: An Overview* (c.2003).

7 *West End Refugee Service* has led the way, followed by the *East Area Asylum Seekers Support Group* and *Walking With* in Wallsend.

8 Julia Darling. 'My Kind of Town.' *Guardian*, 11 September 2004.

9 See Robert Colls & Bill Lancaster (eds). *Geordies; Roots of Regionalism* (Newcastle upon Tyne, Northumbria University Press, 2005, second edition).

10 House of Lords. *Hansard Index*, 8 Nov 2004: Column 681.

11 Ali Madanipour and Tanya Merridew. 'Neighbourhood Governance: Capacity for Social Integration. Newcastle upon Tyne, Walker Case Study'. December 2002 (see website for this project involving 10 European Countries www.infra.kth.se/sb/sp/forskning/index.html – viewed 26 July 2006).

12 *Newcastle Partnership Handbook. Working to Plan*. August 2004 (see www.newcastleplan.org.uk – viewed 2 May 2006).

13 See www.nsp.org.uk – viewed on 2 May 2006.

14 See www.ntsp-online.org.uk – viewed on 2 May 2006.

15 Fred Robinson and Keith Shaw. 'Regeneration, Partnerships, 'Community' and Governance in the North East of England.' *Northern Economic Review*. 31. 2001, 4-19.

16 David Byrne. 'The Nature of Post-Industrialism: South Tyneside in the Twenty-First Century'. *Northern Economic Review*. 36. Summer 2005, 1-14.

17 Natasha Vall. 'The Emergence of the Post-Industrial Economy in Newcastle 1914-2000' In Robert Colls & Bill Lancaster (eds). *Newcastle upon Tyne: A Modern History*, 47-70.

18 There are only 157 resident persons per square mile and 200 villages with fewer than 500 residents across the 2000 square miles of Northumberland.

19 See www.ruralvoices.org.uk – viewed 13 July 2006.

20 Interim Regional Tourism Forum. *North East Tourism Strategy 2005-2010* (www.tourismnortheast.co.uk – viewed 26 July 2006).

21 David Byrne. *Understanding the Urban* (Houndmills, Basingstoke, Palgrave, 2001) See chapter 6.

22 Commission on Urban Life and Faith. *Faithful Cities* (London, Church House Publishing/Methodist Publishing, 2006), 25.

23 Commission on Urban Life and Faith. *Faithful Cities*, 54ff. See paragraphs 6.37 to 6.49.

SIX STAINED GLASS AND OTHER FURNISHINGS

1 For evidence of the chief survivals see L.C. Evetts, 'Medieval Painted Glass in Northumberland', *Archæologia Aeliana*, 4, XX (1942), 91-109; also Evetts, 'Sixteenth-Century Heraldic Glass at Earsdon, Northumberland', *A A*, 4.XXXVII (1959), 333-39; also R.J.S. Bertram, 'Notes on the Old Glass in St John's Church, Newcastle-upon-Tyne', *A A*, 3, XIX (1922), 35-49. Seventeenth and eighteenth-century antiquaries often recorded a larger proportion of medieval glazing than survives today. There are contemporary records for the donation of large windows (or at least the stonework for these) e.g. at Tynemouth Priory and St Nicholas, Newcastle. Fragments of stained glass have also been found during excavations at Tynemouth and Brinkburn priories.

2 See S. Baylis, 'Absolute Magic': A Portrait of George III on Glass by James Pearson', *The Journal of Stained Glass*, XXII (1998), 16-30. The eighteenth-century fragments are of delicately coloured enamels on white glass, mixed in with earlier medieval pieces, in a brightly coloured geometrical setting within a tiny single light window at the west end of the north aisle.

3 The repeal in 1845 of the glass excise duty occasioned a massive restructuring of the British glass industry, not least on Tyneside – although its effects on the market for stained glass are not well understood at present; see Catherine Ross, *The Development of the Glass Industry on the Rivers Tyne and Wear, 1700-1900*. (Unpublished PhD. Thesis, The University of Newcastle-upon-Tyne, 1982).

4 The literature on this particular period is still somewhat limited. Useful surveys are Sarah Brown, *Stained Glass. An Illustrated History,* (London, 1992), 127-34; Martin Harrison, *Victorian Stained Glass,* (London 1980), especially 15-25. Jim Cheshire, *Stained Glass and the Victorian Gothic Revival,* (Manchester 2004) is more limited in scope, but contains some useful insights.

5 Of Gibson's other surviving windows in the diocese, the north transept (1848) at Blanchland Abbey (commissioned by Archdeacon Charles Thorp) imitates Florentine fifteenth-century stained glass, whereas that for Gosforth, St Nicholas (*c.*1845, but re-sited at the west end of the south aisle, and provided with new borders by Wailes, *c.*1860?), is in a stiffly neo-Norman idiom, although far less convincing than Wailes's many essays in this style, e.g. Edlingham, St John (1864).

6 In addition, the windows at Simonburn, St Mungo (of various dates, beginning in 1877); St Cuthbert, Greenhead (1879, being the former east windows re-sited to the south side of the nave) and the *Jesse Tree* (1875) at Heddon-on-the-Wall, St Andrew are all excellent examples of early Kempe and Co. glass – on the whole, more varied artistically than the later, rather standardised productions of this firm.

7 Note also the excellent Morris and Co. *Caritas et Fortitudo* (1898) from the demolished St Cuthbert, Newcastle, now in the Laing Art Gallery, Newcastle.

8 The last three examples were executed by the stained glass department of the innovative London-based glass-works of James Powell and Sons (Whitefriars), for whom Wooldridge and Hardgrave regularly acted as freelance designers.

9 Newcastle, St George was designed by the architect/artist/craftsman Thomas Ralph Spence to a commission from the Tyneside ship-builder Charles Mitchell and his artist son, Charles William. The retired ship-owner Sir James Knott (1855-1934) commissioned the Fenham church as a memorial to two of his sons lost in the First World War. The design team was a veritable roll-call of Arts and Crafts talent, including the architects George Jack and Eric Edward Lofting (advised by William Richard Lethaby), with furniture and wood-carving by Lawrence Turner (to designs by Jack) and stained glass by Edward Woore (some also to Jack's design, being his only designs for the medium).

10 *An Túr Gloine* greatly helped raise the international profile of modern Irish stained glass. It was founded in 1903, under the direction of the noted Irish landscapist/portraitist Sarah Purser, as a co-operative of artist-craftsmen and women.

11 1913, 1919 and two of 1921-2 as part of the parish war memorial. Another was contributed by Healey's colleague, Ethel Rhind.

12 Geddes herself held this window in far higher regard than her more famous war memorials for St Bartholomew, Ottawa (1919), and St Martin's Cathedral, Ypres (1934-8).

13 Hatton (1865-1926) became the first principal of the King Edward VII School of Art at Armstrong College. The Shilbottle window was executed to Hatton's designs by Reed Millican and Co. (Newcastle), and is strongly influenced by the stained glass work of his younger colleague, Richard John Stubbington. It is thought to be Hatton's only surviving church window.

14 Sadly, Barber took his own life – aged only 29 – during the course of this commission. Lawrence Lee completed the remaining panels.

15 C.W. Whall, *Stained Glass Work,* (London, 1905), 84. Whall (1849-1924) is usually regarded as a leading member of the English Arts and Crafts movement. His primary concern was to promote stained glass as a valid medium for the creation of modern works of art.

16 The 1848 restoration at Stamfordham was by Benjamin Ferrey. Much of his stained glass was later replaced (by Clayton & Bell and Kempe & Co.), although some of the side windows to the chancel still retain their (silver) stained and painted crown-glass quarries, whose yellow colour was intended to impart an aura of holiness.

17 The theatricality (and sense of Byzantine mystery) of this space was formerly reinforced by the original (now lost) gas *flambeau* light fittings of the chancel and nave aisles.

SEVEN CHURCHYARDS

1 *Hymns for Little Children*, (1848).

2 A useful summary of some of the symbols used on church monuments can be found on the website of the Church Monuments Society: http://freespace.virgin.net/john.bromilow/CMS/newfile21.htm

3 James Deetz and Edwin S. Dethlefsen, 'The Plymouth Colony Archive Project: Death's Head, Cherub, Urn and Willow', *Natural History*, 76(3), 1967, 29-37.

4 Ellen Clark-King makes the point, for example, that belief in life after death gave the women she interviewed in the east end of Newcastle 'a sense of self-worth that provides a basis for action and a foundation for self-determination.' *Theology By Heart: Women, the Church and God* (Peterborough, Epworth, 2004), 181.

EIGHT BELLS IN THE DIOCESE OF NEWCASTLE

1 Morpeth not only has a ring of bells in the Watch Tower owned by the Council, it is now the only place that nightly rings a curfew bell.
2 A ring of six bells at Newburn, St Michael was destroyed by fire, but it is hoped that these will be replaced by December 2007.
3 John Mills still do brass castings at their factory on Shields Road, Newcastle. They have not made a church bell for over a hundred years but they still make the occasional ship's bell.
4 The largest number of bells cast in a set of bells in the area was for the Great North-East Summer Exhibition of 1929. These bells, all 49 of them, definitely had wanderlust. They were cast in Croydon, came to Tyneside for the exhibition, then went to Hyde Park in London and finally ended up travelling across the world to Wellington in New Zealand where they form the First World War Memorial Carillon.

NINE MUSIC IN THE DIOCESE OF NEWCASTLE: A PERSONAL APPRECIATION

1 I live in Bellingham and play many of the organs in the North Tyne and Rede Valleys, and in a 'corridor' from north to south, from Elsdon to Blanchland. In commenting on church music outside this area, I would like to thank the RSCM in Northumbria and the Newcastle & District Society of Organists, and am indebted to the information held on the British Institute of Organ Studies website. This website also contains detailed information about a number of organs within the diocese.
2 Other notable organs include those at Gosforth, St Nicholas, Gosforth, All Saints, Newcastle, St George (Jesmond) and Newcastle, St Gabriel (Heaton) – but the list of fine instruments is surprisingly long. The gazetteer in this book includes brief notes on most of them (ed.).

TEN GAZETTEER

1 John Grundy, Grace McCombie, Peter Ryder, Humphrey Welfare and Nikolaus Pevsner, *The Buildings of England: Northumberland* (London, Penguin, 1992).
2 S. Prins and R. Massingberd-Mundy (eds), *Guide to the Anglican Churches in Newcastle and Northumberland* (Newcastle, Bishop's Editorial Committee, 1982).
3 Simon Jenkins, *England's Thousand Best Churches* (London, Allen Lane, 1999), 504
4 www.newcastle.anglican.org
5 Simon Jenkins, *England's Thousand Best Churches*, 504.

GLOSSARY

APSE	Semi-circular extension – in a church almost always at the east end of a chancel.
ARCADE	A series of arches supported by piers or column – in a church it usually divides the nave from the aisles.
BELLCOTE	A small (often gabled) belfry – usually housing just one or two bells.
CAPITAL	The (sometimes decorated) head of a column.
CHANCEL	The east end of a church – sometimes also called the 'choir' – in which the main altar stands.
FUNERARY HATCHMENT	A coat of arms on a lozenge-shaped frame.
LANCET WINDOW	A tall, slender, single light window with a pointed arch.
LYCH-GATE	A roofed gate at the entrance to a churchyard – where a coffin may be received before a funeral service.
NARTHEX	It may sound like a pretentious name for an annexe, but it is properly a covered porch or vestibule at the main entrance to a church.
NAVE	The main body of a church.
PARVISE	Either another name for a narthex (see above) or, as at Warkworth, a room over a church.
PELE (OR PEEL)	A stone tower house.
PISCINA	Basin (usually stone) for washing communion vessels.
QUOINS	Dressed stones at the corner of a building.
RESPOND	A half-column, usually set into a wall – it usually carries an arch.
REREDOS	Screen behind an altar – often carved or painted.
SEDILIA	Stone seats for priests, set into the south side of a chancel wall.
SPRINGER	The first (bottom) stones of an arch or vault.
SQUINT	An aperture affording a view of an altar.
TRANSEPT	The 'arms' of a cross-shaped church.
VOUSSOIR	The wedge-shaped stones of an arch.

BRIEF BIOGRAPHIES OF THE CONTRIBUTORS

CHRISTOPHER DALLISTON

Christopher Dalliston was brought up in Norfolk and ordained in 1984. During his ministry he has served in parishes in the Essex countryside, the East End of London and as incumbent of Boston in Lincolnshire, a parish including St Botolph's Church (affectionately known as 'the Stump'), one of the largest and most glorious Parish Churches in England. He became Dean of Newcastle in 2003. The development of Church buildings and their appropriate use and adaptation for use by the wider community have featured high in his ministry, including the re-development of St Edmund's, Forest Gate and the building of a new Church Centre in Boston. The renewal of the fabric, infrastructure and mission of St Nicholas is very much on the Cathedral's agenda.

CHRISTOPHER LEWIS

Christopher Lewis was ordained in Newcastle in 1967 and returned to the diocese in 2001, as priest in Riding Mill, chaplain to Shepherds Dene, and Adviser in Spiritual Direction. In the meantime he had been a missionary in Borneo, a Vicar in Luton and then Whitstable and a Residentiary Canon and Officer for Ministry and Training in Bradford Diocese. He prepared for theological college by working with refugee Tibetan lamas in the Himalayas, and increasingly finds wood carving and music as much a route to the mystery of God as theology, sacrament and scripture.

CES MADDISON

Ces Maddison is Director of Design at Architects Purves Ash LLP based in Newcastle upon Tyne. After studying architecture in London and Nottingham he returned with his family to the North-East in 1976. Ces has sustained a lifelong interest in drawing and sketching both professionally and for fun. Ces is Chairman of Northern Print, an open access studio and gallery promoting excellence in print-making for the North-East Region. As a Fellow of the Royal Society of Arts he believes strongly in social values and fostering resilient communities.

EILEEN McLEAN

Eileen McLean was born in Newcastle and grew up in County Durham. After a very short career as a mathematician, she spent over 20 years at home bringing up a family, during which time she was actively involved in the local community, overseas and homelessness charities, and the Church, mainly in the area of adult education. She was ordained Deacon in 1988 and served as a curate in Burley-in-wharfedale in Bradford Diocese. In 1992 she went to St Peter's church in the middle of Nottingham as Associate Rector, and for five years was also Area Dean of Central Nottingham Deanery. In 2002, it was back to the great contrast of the rural North-East. Eileen is now Vicar of Bamburgh and Ellingham, with the added responsibility of developing the Church's ministry to visitors, in the deaneries of Bamburgh & Glendale and Norham.

NEIL MOAT

Born in 1959, Neil Moat studied at Newcastle University. He writes (and lectures) as an art historian on nineteenth and twentieth-century ecclesiastical architecture and decorative arts, with a specialist interest in stained glass and the British *Arts and Crafts* movement, as represented in the North-East of England. He is a member of the Advisory Committees for the Care of Churches of the Anglican dioceses of Durham and Newcastle, and the Historic Churches Committee of the Roman Catholic Diocese of Hexham and Newcastle.

GEOFFREY PURVES

Geoffrey Purves is Chairman of Purves Ash LLP, a firm of architects in Newcastle upon Tyne. He has held a range of professional appointments with the Royal Institute of British Architects and is an Honorary Research Associate at Durham University. Currently he is Chairman of the Diocesan Advisory Committee and has overseen the production of this book along with the other contributors.

PETER ROBINSON

Peter Robinson grew up in south London. He read Natural Sciences at Cambridge and trained in Durham for ordination in the Church of England. After serving his curacy in the North Shields Team, he moved to Byker in 1999 to be Director of the Urban Ministry and Theology Project of the Newcastle East Deanery. The project serves local churches by assisting them to engage with social and economic regeneration and, from this engagement, to discover appropriate ways of being a church within fast changing communities. Peter teaches urban theology, and also Anglicanism and spirituality, on courses validated by Durham University and delivered within the Newcastle diocese.

JOHN ROPER

John Roper studied music at the Royal Academy of Music. Until he moved to Northumberland in 2001 he was director of music in a number of Essex churches (latterly at St Mary's, Theydon Bois), and conducted a number of secular and sacred choirs. As an organist, he has played in many UK churches and cathedrals. He now plays for churches in and around Bellingham and Hexham, and conducts the North Tyne and Redewater Choral Society and the chamber choir 'Antiphon'

HELEN SAVAGE

Helen Savage is a full-time writer and adult educator and also an Anglican priest. She trained as an archaeologist and directed excavations on Hadrian's Wall. She is wine correspondent of *The Journal* and a Member of the Circle of Wine Writers. She has also written about adult learning, music, theology and gender studies. After a curacy in Heaton, she served as Adult Educator Adviser in the diocese of Newcastle and then as Vicar of Bedlington.

HOWARD SMITH

Howard Smith was taught to ring at St Michael's, Basingstoke in 1964 and has since rung bells at churches all over the British Isles. He came to the North-East in 1972 and lives and works in Killingworth. He is a member of the Newcastle Cathedral Society of Bellringers and is passionately interested in all aspects relating to the history of bells in the old counties of Northumberland and Durham. He is 'Bell Maintenance Adviser' for the Durham and Newcastle Diocesan Association of Church Bellringers and also advises both dioceses on any matters regarding bell installations.

CYRIL WINSKELL

Cyril was born in 1932 in North Shields. After being articled to a South Shields architect, he continued his studies at King's College, Newcastle. Cyril has a special interest in city and townscape and in conservation architecture and has enjoyed a long and highly distinguished career based in the North-East. His projects have included acting as Consultant Architect to Liverpool Housing Trust; the restoration of the historic hospital streets in Newcastle Royal Victoria Infirmary and the conservation and restoration of Mitford Castle, Northumberland. A fine painter, he has exhibited many times at the Royal Academy Summer Exhibition.

IAN WOOD

Ian Wood is Professor of Early Medieval History at the University of Leeds. He has published widely on the Early Middle Ages, including books on *The Merovingian Kingdoms 450-751* (London, 1994) and *The Missionary Life, Saints and the Evangelisation of Europe* (London, 2001). He has also written a large number of articles on Anglo-Saxon History, including *The Most Holy Abbot Ceolfrid*, which was the Jarrow Lecture for 1995, and 'Bede's Jarrow', in *A Place to Believe In: Locating Medieval Landscapes*, edited by Clare Lees and Gillian Overing (University Park, Pennsylvania, 2006). Among his current projects is a commentary on Bede's Life of the Abbots of Wearmouth and Jarrow.

SPONSORS

Thanks go to the following individuals and organisations who have kindly made donations to assist with the cost of colour printing. Their support is greatly appreciated.

B. T. Bell Consulting Engineers
Benfield
Carillion Regional Building
Ecclesiastical Insurance Group
Historic Property Restoration Ltd
J. Barbour & Son Limited
Closegate Projects Ltd
Lord & Lady Stevens
Patrick Parsons Ltd
Purves Ash LLP
Ryecroft Glenton
Sintons LLP
Sir Robert McAlpine Ltd
Tony Atkinson & Associates
Ward Hadaway
Watson Burton LLP

INDEX

If you are interested in purchasing other books published by Tempus, or in case you have difficulty finding any Tempus books in your local bookshop, you can also place orders directly through our website

www.tempus-publishing.com